Holiday Fun
Year-Round
with
DIAN
THOMAS

Holiday Fun
Year-Round
with
DIAN
THOMAS

DEDICATION

Dedicated to Woody Fraser, producer of the ABC *Home* show, whose vision and creativity are unmatched.

Holiday Fun Year-Round with Dian Thomas. Copyright ©1995 by Dian Thomas. All rights reserved. No part of this book may be reproduced in any form or by any means without the prior written permission of the publisher. Published by The Dian Thomas Company, P.O. Box 171107, Holladay, UT 84117. 1-800-846-6355. First Edition.

Printing 10 9 8 7 6 5 4 3 2 1

Library of Congress Catalog-in-Publication Data
Thomas, Dian
    Holiday Fun Year-Round with Dian Thomas

ISBN: 0-9621257-2-5

Main entry under title: Holiday Fun Year-Round with Dian Thomas
Includes Index.
1. Holidays
2. Holidays—Crafts
3. Holidays—Cookbook

Editors
    Deanna DeLong
    Marla Wells
    Dianne King

Art Director and Illustrator
    DeeAnn Thaxton

Photographers
    Brian Tweed
    Borge Andersen
    Dian Thomas

Cover and Interior Designer
    Sandy Kent

Designer
    Cathleen Carbery-Shaw

ACKNOWLEDGMENTS

This book is based on twenty years' experience of sharing creative ideas about how to have fun with your friends and family. It is also the result of a great effort by many people who deserve a special thanks.

I appreciate the unflagging support I've received from Budge Wallis, who has always believed in me and continually encouraged me to share my novel ideas with others. Rick Bailey is another dear friend whose early belief in me provided the motivation to start my own publishing company.

DeeAnn Thaxton deserves a gold medal for her tireless help in creating, illustrating, and making countless crafts and projects. Her energy, talent, imagination, and ability to execute my ideas have nurtured my own creative process! Brenda Carver has provided wonderful assistance with the crafts and photography.

Many thanks to Woody Fraser, the producer from the ABC *Home* show, and Steve Friedman, from the NBC *Today* show, who gave me a window of opportunity to showcase my ideas on national television in front of millions of viewers for fourteen years.

I would like to thank Barbara Dahl, Sue Allison, and Floss Waltman for their caring and friendship. Support from my family has also been never-ending.

I'm grateful to Catherine Brohaugh for getting this project off the ground by taking my ideas and organizing them. Shannon Harmon has also been a great support.

Dianne King, my longtime friend and editor, has again given her best on this project. Her expertise and eye for error have been essential in the final proofreading. Mike Tuskes' thorough research is appreciated, and Eva Garlick's help with the final editing was vital.

Sandy Kent provided the excellent layout design for the book, to which Cathleen Carbery-Shaw skillfully applied her artistic abilities. Cathleen's superb design work, resourcefulness, flexibility, and perseverance made the book come to life and gave it color.

Last, but not least, I want to thank Deanna DeLong and Marla Wells for meticulously editing the manuscript and executing every detail to completion. Their ingenuity, dedication, and diligence have been indispensable.

JANUARY

FEBRUARY

MARCH

APRIL

MAY

JUNE

JULY

AUGUST

SEPTEMBER

OCTOBER

NOVEMBER

DECEMBER

Preface

Holiday Fun Year-Round is about enjoying more of the simple fun in life with the people who matter the most. Holidays provide the perfect excuse to step out of the everyday hustle and bustle and create some enjoyment for yourself and your family and friends.

Many people ask me where my ideas come from. I'm sometimes characterized as being a well of creativity that never seems to run dry. My creativity has sprung from the need to problem-solve. For fourteen years, when I was appearing on the NBC *Today* show and the ABC *Home* show, the problem was to come up with new ideas for the show every week! This made me stretch my thinking and perspective. Creativity became a habit that is now part of me. I search for new ideas everywhere I go, and I'm always on the lookout for anything simple and clever.

You can tap into your store of creativity as well! Listen and continually expose yourself to new ways of doing things. Watch for ideas that transform ordinary items or tools into something else. Try a new approach to an old task. You'll surprise your family, your friends, and yourself!

The ideas in this book are simple. They are simple enough so that children and adults can enjoy them together. They are simple enough to be fun instead of stressful. They are simple enough to be a springboard for your own creative ideas. They are simple so that you can focus on the enjoyment you'll have doing them and sharing them with others.

As well as fresh ideas for celebrating, decorating, and cooking, you will also find interesting information about American holidays included with each month. Again, this is meant to spark your interest in knowing more about the origins of our traditional holidays. Sometimes these facts are just interesting trivia, and sometimes they deepen our love for our country and culture.

There is a year's worth of festive fun in *Holiday Fun Year-Round*, but take your time in trying it all. Remember that there will always be another holiday! I hope that you'll have as much fun using these ideas as I've had creating them. Enjoy!

—Dian Thomas

JANUARY

January's here, and it's time to celebrate and de-stress from the Thanksgiving and Christmas holidays! The New Year brings many opportunities for parties, good wishes, resolutions, and family togetherness, despite the chill outdoors.

New Year's Eve entertaining is fun and easy with the decorations and recipes in this chapter. Make a time capsule while you're waiting for the New Year to arrive. There's even a way to redecorate your Christmas tree for New Year's Eve.

New Year's Day is for relaxation and reflection. There's an easy-to-make, yet elegant, breakfast that will allow you time to start on those resolutions you made the night before. If you need more munchies to make it through all of today's bowl games, look ahead to the Super Bowl Sunday recipes.

The anniversary of Martin Luther King, Jr.'s, birth is increasingly observed throughout the country. His dream was to see this nation live out its creed that all men are created equal. This holiday is a time for commemoration and rededication to the goal of equal rights for all Americans.

Send January out in style with a Super Bowl party your friends will get a kick out of. Root your favorite team to victory with great food served on a table that looks like a football field.

New Year's Eve

The Romans first called January 1 the new year back in 153 B.C. Then in the Middle Ages, Christians changed it to December 25, the traditional date of Jesus' birth. Later it was changed to March 25, the Annunciation. During the 16th century, Pope Gregory XIII changed the calendar again and returned the new year to January 1.

All over the world, people celebrate the end of the old year and the arrival of the new one. Many superstitions mark the beginning of the new year. In the South, it's good luck to eat black-eyed peas on New Year's Day.

When you enter a person's house for the first time in the new year in Scotland, you should bring a lump of coal and a piece of bread so that your friends will be warm and well fed that year. In Spain, eating 12 grapes at the new year brings good luck for the next 12 months.

Millions of people watch the Tournament of Roses Parade in Pasadena, California, on New Year's Day, a tradition since 1886. On New Year's afternoon, one of the biggest college football games of the year is played at the Rose Bowl, not far from the parade route.

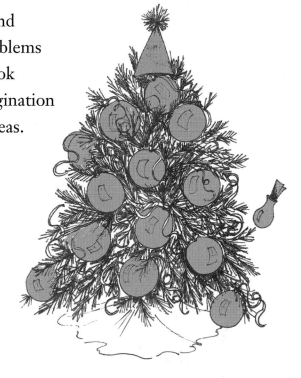

Ring in the New Year with these great food and decorating ideas. It's time to release the problems of the past year like helium-filled balloons and look ahead to possibilities of the future. Use your imagination and don't be afraid to have fun with these zany ideas.

GOOD FORTUNE TREE

Don't take down that Christmas tree yet. Turn it into a fun New Year's decoration!

Leftover Christmas tree, undecorated
Balloons, 6" to 8"
Chinese fortunes or wishes, typed on small pieces of paper
One-dollar bills
Ribbon
String confetti
Happy New Year's hat

Remove the Christmas ornaments and lights from your tree and replace them with small balloons filled with New Year's wishes, Chinese fortunes, and dollar bills. Place the wish, fortune, or money inside the uninflated balloon and blow it up.

Tie the balloons to the tree with ribbon, being careful not to pop them. Finish decorating the tree with string confetti and a Happy New Year's hat.

As the New Year rings in, guests can pop the balloons and claim the wishes, fortunes, and money inside. Your guests will love this unique twist on the party favor.

NOISEMAKERS

These noisemakers are far more entertaining than the ones you can buy in the store!

Use a two-liter plastic pop bottle filled with small buttons or dry beans to make a New Year's noisemaker. Decorate the outside of each bottle with felt, lace, buttons, ribbons, and bows. The bottle neck makes the handle.

Another idea is to put a few dry beans or small rocks in an empty aluminum pop can and tape the hole shut. Cut a piece of wrapping paper twice as wide as the circumference of the can. Roll the can in the paper, secure with tape, and tie the ends with ribbon.

NEW YEAR'S TIME CAPSULE

Freeze time for your family.

Obtain coffee cans or wide-mouth glass jars with lids for each family member. To individualize each time capsule, draw faces with permanent markers and glue on yarn hair.

Place all the capsules in a cardboard box, seal with tape, and decorate. Write "Do Not Open 'til 2000" (or whatever year you decide) on the outside. Put in a secure place in the attic or basement.

HERBED CHEESE DIP

This dip stores well in the refrigerator for up to a week.

1 clove garlic
1 (8 ounce) package low-fat cream cheese
1/2 teaspoon tarragon
1/4 teaspoon basil
1/4 teaspoon thyme
1/4 teaspoon oregano
1/4 teaspoon salt
3 tablespoons low-fat sour cream

Mince garlic in food processor fitted with steel blade. Add remaining ingredients except sour cream and process until smooth. Add sour cream and pulse. (The sour cream will become runny if overblended.) Place in serving container.

Serve with thin flatbread crackers, bread sticks, raw vegetables, or fresh fruits.

CRANBERRY ICE

Fresh cranberries will keep well in the refrigerator for up to two months.

1 (12 ounce) package fresh cranberries
2 cups sugar
1 quart water
Juice of 3 lemons
1 teaspoon grated orange peel

Boil cranberries, sugar, and 2 cups water together in a saucepan until berries pop. Process in a blender until smooth. Add lemon juice, 2 cups water, and orange peel.

Freeze in a plastic container. Remove from the freezer about 1 hour before serving. Slush with a fork or in the blender. Serves 4 to 6.

You might want to include things like:

- favorite photos
- newspaper articles
- baseball cards
- lists of your favorite foods, books, movies, TV shows, etc.
- a list of goals
- a lock of hair

New Year's Day

New Year's morning is generally a time to relax and recover from the night before. It takes a lot of energy to think about making all those resolutions! Start your New Year off right with an easy but delicious breakfast. These quick snacks will keep everyone happy and satisfied whether you're watching football, curling up with a favorite book, or enjoying time with the family.

To ensure good luck throughout the year, fill all your salt shakers on New Year's Day from a fresh box of salt.

GERMAN PANCAKES

This fluffy pancake should be eaten as soon as it comes out of the oven!

1 cup milk
1 cup all-purpose flour
6 large eggs
Dash salt
1 teaspoon vanilla
4 tablespoons butter or margarine
Topping

Preheat oven to 400°F. Mix milk, flour, eggs, salt, and vanilla in a blender until smooth. Melt 1 tablespoon butter or margarine in each of four 9″ pie pans in oven. Remove pans as soon as butter melts and tilt to grease entire pan.

Divide batter into each of the four pie pans. Bake 10 to 15 minutes or until golden brown. The edges will puff up, and the pancake will form a well in the center. Remove from oven when golden and serve immediately. Serves 4.

TOPPING

1 (10 ounce) box frozen raspberries, slightly thawed
1 (20 ounce) can chunk pineapple, drained
4 bananas
1/2 cup firmly packed brown sugar
1 (8 ounce) container dairy sour cream

Spoon raspberries, pineapple, and bananas into the center of pancake. Sprinkle with brown sugar and top with sour cream.

HOT GRAPE PUNCH

This favorite summertime cooler is totally different when heated and served in mugs.

6 cups water
1 quart unsweetened grape juice
1 (6 ounce) can frozen lemonade concentrate
1 (6 ounce) can frozen orange juice concentrate
Orange slices for garnish

Mix ingredients in a 4-quart saucepan. Heat until warm and serve in mugs, garnished with orange slices. Makes 12 cups.

TV MUNCHIES

This traditional favorite is great for snacking while you're watching bowl games.

1/4 cup butter or margarine
4 teaspoons Worcestershire sauce
1 teaspoon seasoning salt
6 cups wheat, corn, or rice cereal
3/4 cup salted nuts
1 cup pretzels

Preheat oven to 250°F. In a large saucepan, melt butter or margarine; stir in Worcestershire sauce and salt. Add cereal, nuts, and pretzels; stir until all the pieces are coated. Spread the mixture out in a 10″ x 15″ pan. Bake for 30 to 45 minutes, stirring every 15 minutes until crisp.

Place on paper towels to cool. Serve immediately or place in tightly covered containers for gifts or storage. Makes 7 cups.

New Year's Day Refreshers

Try some of these tasty snacks:

- Hot cider
- Low-fat cheese slices and crackers
- Breadsticks
- Sliced crisp vegetables with ranch dressing or cottage cheese blended smooth
- Dried fruit with nuts, wheat nuts, sunflower seeds, and coconut flakes
- Deviled eggs
- Granola
- Tomato juice with a dash of onion salt and lemon juice, served with a stick of celery
- Celery stuffed with peanut butter and raisins or nuts
- Celery stuffed with low-fat pineapple, strawberry, or chive cream cheese

Martin Luther King, Jr.'s, Birthday

THIRD MONDAY IN JANUARY

Martin Luther King, Jr., was born on January 15, 1929, in Atlanta, Georgia. As a boy, he realized that Southern blacks were denied many of the basic human rights which white people enjoyed. Recognizing that a good education was the key to his own personal success, he received a bachelor's degree in sociology, then studied to be a minister, and later received his PhD degree.

Martin Luther King, Jr., led nonviolent protests against segregation, hoping to get discriminatory laws changed. He staged marches, boycotts, and protests, trying to keep them nonviolent. He was awarded the Nobel Peace Prize in 1964, the youngest man ever to receive it. His life came to a tragic end on April 4, 1968, when he was shot and killed outside his hotel room in Memphis, Tennessee.

In 1986, President Ronald Reagan and Congress created a new national holiday which celebrated King's birthday, recognizing his work to bring equal rights to the disadvantaged, the poor, and blacks. Congress debated whether or not this should be a national holiday for over 15 years. Our celebration of his birth is a tribute to this great man and his contributions toward equal rights for all.

"I Have A Dream"

"I have a dream that one day this nation will rise up and live out the true meaning of its creed: 'We hold these truths to be self-evident, that all men are created equal.'

"I have a dream that one day on the red hills of Georgia the sons of former slaves and the sons of former slave-owners will be able to sit down together at the table of brotherhood. . . .

"I have a dream that my four little children will one day live in a nation where they will not be judged by the color of their skin but by the content of their character.

"I have a dream today.

"I have a dream that one day . . . little black boys and black girls will be able to join hands with little white boys and white girls as sisters and brothers.

"I have a dream today. . . .

"When we let freedom ring, when we let it ring from every village and every hamlet, from every state and every city, we will be able to speed up that day when all of God's children, black men and white men, Jews and Gentiles, Protestants and Catholics, will be able to join hands and sing in the words of the old Negro spiritual, 'Free at last! Free at last! Thank God almighty, we are free at last!'"

Martin Luther King, Jr.'s, birthday celebrates the life and contributions of this social peacemaker and civil rights leader. It's a time to reflect on ways each of us can reach out to others in peace and brotherhood.

Take some time today for kindness. Visit a nursing home and talk with a resident. Shovel snow from your neighbor's walkway. Be a courteous driver. Every kind act you do anonymously counts for three that are known. You can probably think of a dozen other ways your kind actions can bring peace into the hearts of others.

PEACE CARROT CAKE

Just as Martin Luther King, Jr., brought all kinds of people together in peace and love, this carrot cake combines a variety of different ingredients for a scrumptious dessert.

2 cups all-purpose flour
1 cup granulated sugar
1 cup brown sugar, firmly packed
2 teaspoons baking powder
1 teaspoon salt
2 teaspoons baking soda
2 teaspoons cinnamon
1/2 teaspoon nutmeg
4 eggs
1-1/2 cups canola oil
3 cups shredded carrots
1 cup chopped walnuts or pecans
Cream Cheese Frosting

Preheat oven to 350°F. Generously grease and flour 1 large 9″ x 12″ x 2″ baking pan. In a large bowl, combine flour, sugars, baking powder, salt, baking soda, cinnamon, and nutmeg. In a small bowl, beat eggs and oil. Add to flour mixture. Mix with electric mixer on low speed until blended. Fold in carrots and chopped nuts. Pour into prepared baking pan.

Bake 25 to 30 minutes or until wooden pick inserted in center comes out clean. Cool in pan on rack 10 minutes. Turn out onto rack to cool completely. Frost with Cream Cheese Frosting.

Have a Dream

Check out Martin Luther King's recording "I Have a Dream" from your local library. After listening to it, have each person in your family make a list of dreams for a better world. Discuss each individual family member's list, and then compile a family list to make things better for your neighborhood, your city, or the world.

From your dream list, make an action list of things you can do now to start making those dreams come true.

CREAM CHEESE FROSTING

1 (8 ounce) package cream cheese, room temperature
1/2 cup butter, room temperature
2 teaspoons vanilla extract
1 (1 pound) box powdered sugar

In a medium bowl, beat cream cheese and butter until fluffy. Blend in vanilla. Gradually add powdered sugar, beating until smooth and creamy. Spread frosting over sides and top of cake.

Super Bowl Sunday

Super Bowl Sunday isn't technically a holiday, but perhaps it should be! It's a great day for friends to get together and, of course, to root for a favorite team.

FOOTBALL FIELD TABLE

Your guests will have as much fun looking at this table as they will watching the Super Bowl!

Green tablecloth
Ruler
Pencil
White contact paper
4 large gumdrops
4 straws
2 pipe cleaners
2 football helmets
Spray paint
2 pink or brown balloons
Felt scraps
Low-heat glue gun or double-stick tape

Cover the table with the green tablecloth. Using a ruler and pencil, mark each 10-yard line. Cut strips of contact paper as long as your table is wide, using the guidelines on the back of the paper. The number and width of the strips will be determined by the size of your tablecloth. Peel off the backing and place crosswise on the green tablecloth to look like a football field. If you have a large enough table, cut numbers from the contact paper to indicate yard lines.

Push a straw into each of the gumdrops. Twist one end of a pipe cleaner three-quarters up one straw, then twist the other end around a second straw, forming a goalpost. Repeat the process so that you have one goalpost at each end of the table.

Spray paint the helmets the colors of the Super Bowl teams. Blow up the balloons and gently push them into the helmets to form heads. Sketch facial features (eyes, brows, nose, and lips) on paper, then place on felt and cut out. Carefully glue the features on the balloons with a low-temperature glue gun or double-stick tape.

9

TOUCHDOWN POPCORN

Use a hot-air corn popper for fat-free popcorn.

10 cups popped popcorn
1/2 cup chopped nuts (optional)
1 cup dark brown sugar (packed)
1/2 cup light corn syrup
1 tablespoon butter
1/2 teaspoon salt
1/4 teaspoon baking soda

Preheat oven to 250°F. Place popcorn and nuts in an extra-large bowl and set aside.

In a heavy medium-sized saucepan, combine sugar, corn syrup, butter, and salt. Bring to a boil, stirring to dissolve sugar. Cook for 2 or 3 minutes, until the mixture reaches 250°F, the hard-ball stage. (At the hard-ball stage, a few drops of syrup dropped into cold water form a hard ball.)

Remove pan from heat and stir in baking soda. Pour the mixture over the popcorn and nuts, stirring until kernels are coated evenly. Place in 2 or 3 large oblong baking pans. Bake for 30 minutes, stirring every 10 minutes. Makes 10 cups.

POPCORN FOOTBALLS

These are as fun to make as they are to eat!!

1/4 cup chunky peanut butter
1 (10 ounce) package large marshmallows
1 (12 ounce) bag chocolate chips
7 cups popped popcorn
Black string licorice
2 tablespoons soft butter

Warm peanut butter on low in microwave for 1 minute. In another bowl, melt marshmallows and chocolate chips in microwave on low for 1 minute. Stir marshmallow and chocolate chip mixture into soft peanut butter. Pour over popped popcorn in very large bowl and stir to coat popcorn with mixture.

Rub hands with softened butter and shape popcorn into football shapes, 8″ long x 5″ in diameter. Cut black string licorice and press into footballs for laces. Makes 3 footballs.

FOOTBALL HOAGIE

Pack slices of this bread with your favorite sandwich fillings, serve with Caesar Salad, or scoop out and fill with soup or chili.

3 loaves frozen whole wheat bread dough
1 egg
1 tablespoon water

Thaw the bread dough until pliable, according to package directions. Remove 1/3 from the end of each loaf. Combine two of the 1/3 pieces and set the third piece aside.

Mold each of the four larger pieces of bread dough into a football shape, about 10″ long, by turning ends underneath and tapering.

From the remaining dough, form a long, thin rope, about 1/4″ in diameter. Lay a 4″ long piece lengthwise on each football. Lay three 1-1/2″ long pieces across each long piece to look like the stitching on a football. Secure the stitching on each end with wooden picks.

In small bowl, beat egg with 1 tablespoon water. Brush on footballs with pastry brush. Cover and allow the dough to rise until double in size.

Preheat oven to 350°F. Bake raised loaves for 20 minutes, or until golden brown.

To serve, set out trays of sandwich makings (meat, cheese, lettuce, tomatoes, onions, dressing, etc.) and let everyone help themselves, or slice and serve with Caesar Salad. You can also slice the footballs in half, hollow the insides, and use as soup or chili bowls. Makes 4 footballs.

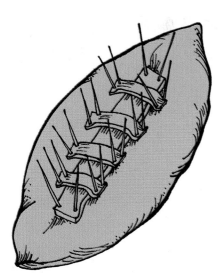

SAUCY CHILI

Saucy and spicy, this chili is perfect for a cold winter day when topped with Cheddar cheese or the Spicy Sour Cream Topping.

1 tablespoon extra-light olive oil
1 pound extra-lean ground beef
1 large onion, chopped
1 medium green pepper, coarsely chopped
2 cloves garlic, minced
2 teaspoons chili powder
1/8 teaspoon cayenne pepper
1/8 teaspoon paprika
1 teaspoon salt
1 (1 pound, 12 ounce) can stewed tomatoes,
    undrained
1 (8 ounce) can tomato sauce
2 (15-1/2 ounce) cans kidney beans, drained
3/4 pound Cheddar cheese, shredded
Spicy Sour Cream Topping

Sauté ground beef in olive oil until brown in large frying pan. Add chopped onion, pepper, and garlic. Transfer to large Dutch oven or stockpot. Add spices, stewed tomatoes, and tomato sauce.

Bring mixture to a boil and simmer for 1 to 1-1/2 hours, stirring occasionally. Add beans and heat. Serve in football bowls with shredded Cheddar cheese and/or Spicy Sour Cream Topping. Serves 6 to 8.

SPICY SOUR CREAM TOPPING

1 (8 ounce) carton low-fat sour cream
1/3 cup red salsa
1/2 teaspoon chili powder
1/2 teaspoon onion powder
1 tablespoon lemon juice
1 teaspoon Dijon mustard

In medium bowl, combine all ingredients. Stir until well mixed.

There are no limitations to what you can do, except the limitations of your own mind as to what you cannot do. Don't think you cannot; think you can.

SUNDAY CAESAR SALAD

This popular salad is best when made with freshly grated Parmesan cheese.

4 thick slices French bread, cut into 3/4" cubes
2 cloves garlic, crushed
8 cups torn Romaine lettuce
Caesar Dressing
1/4 cup finely shredded Parmesan cheese

Preheat oven to 350°F. Combine bread cubes and crushed garlic in a large zip-top plastic bag. Seal bag; shake to coat bread cubes. Spread bread cubes in a jelly roll pan and bake for 10 to 15 minutes or until toasted and golden.

In large bowl, toss lettuce and Caesar Dressing. Top with croutons and shredded Parmesan cheese. Serves 6 to 8.

CAESAR DRESSING

2 large cloves garlic
2 tablespoons Dijon mustard
1-1/2 teaspoons Worcestershire sauce
3 tablespoons lemon juice
1 tablespoon red wine vinegar
1/4 cup extra light olive oil
1/2 teaspoon freshly ground pepper
1/3 cup freshly grated Parmesan cheese

In food processor, combine salad dressing ingredients. Process until smooth and thick.

DILLED SHRIMP DIP

Use crackers or fresh vegetables to scoop up this flavorful dip.

1 (8 ounce) package low-fat cream cheese, softened
1/4 cup fresh lemon juice (1 lemon)
1 pound shrimp, cooked, peeled, and coarsely chopped
1/2 cup finely chopped green onions
1/2 cup reduced-calorie mayonnaise
1/2 cup low-fat sour cream
1 tablespoon Worcestershire sauce
1/2 teaspoon dried dill weed
Hot sauce or ground cayenne pepper
Salt

Mix cream cheese and lemon juice together in a medium bowl. Stir in shrimp and green onions. Add mayonnaise, sour cream, Worcestershire sauce, and dill. Add hot sauce or ground cayenne pepper and salt to taste. Turn mixture into a serving dish and chill.

ORANGE FROST

Try this refreshing drink instead of orange juice for breakfast.

1 (6 ounce) can frozen orange juice concentrate
1 cup low-fat milk
1/2 cup water
8 ice cubes
1 teaspoon vanilla
Orange slices

Place all ingredients except orange slices in blender. Blend until smooth. Garnish with fresh orange slices. Serves 2 to 3.

FEBRUARY

February tends to be the forgotten month because it's so short, but it has some fun holidays. Blast the winter blahs and take time to celebrate.

The Chinese New Year is a wonderful opportunity for gathering with family and friends to share age-old oriental traditions. The Fire-Breathing Dragon looks a little complex, but it's not, and it will delight your family!

Of course, there's Valentine's Day, set aside to show love and affection for the important people in your life. This chapter is filled with Valentine treats that will delight everyone. Nothing shows how much you care like a handmade gift, even a gift simple enough for your little one to make.

Presidents' Day is more than just a day off from work. It's a day to celebrate the contributions of two of our country's greatest leaders. Make a special dessert on this special holiday to remind yourself and your family how great it is to live in America.

Once every four years we get an extra day! Do something weird and backward to celebrate Leap Year.

So enjoy February! It may be cold and gloomy out, but indoors, you'll have fun and fellowship as you celebrate these holidays.

Chinese New Year

BETWEEN JANUARY 21ST AND FEBRUARY 19TH

The Chinese New Year usually falls between January 21st and February 19th, based on the lunar Chinese calendar. In areas where many Chinese-Americans live, the day is celebrated with a spectacular parade with brilliant floats and costumes, musical instruments, whistles, and cymbals. Usually there is a long dragon that weaves from side to side, blowing flames and smoke from its nostrils. Parade watchers throw gifts of money wrapped in red paper, and the men inside the dragon scramble to pick them up. Fireworks explode throughout the day and into the night. The air is filled with the smell of gunpowder mingled with the spicy fragrance of incense sticks. The celebration ends with banquets, payment of debts, and more fireworks.

The Chinese New Year is a great opportunity to show off your creative side. The decorations and food of a traditional Chinese New Year are flamboyant, dramatic, and great fun for the family to make together.

FIRE-BREATHING DRAGON

This dragon is as fun to make as it is to look at!

2 (18 ounce) and 2 (36 ounce) empty round oatmeal boxes
1 sheet of posterboard
2 yards cream-colored self-adhesive paper
Bright green fluorescent spray paint
1 yard wide yellow rickrack
2 large wiggly eyes or black buttons
2 large orange pom-poms
1/4 yard dark red felt
1-1/2" wide dark green plastic tape
Scissors
Glue gun
Glue sticks
Custard cup
Dry ice

Remove lids from the oatmeal boxes. Cut two dragon wings from the posterboard, leaving at least a 1″ flap to attach them to the dragon. Spray paint the wings, the bottoms of all the boxes, and the self-adhesive paper with green paint. The paint does not have to be smooth—splotches of light and dark green give a nice dragon effect. When dry, cover the boxes with painted paper.

Cut a mouth from the closed end of one of the large boxes by cutting two triangles from the sides, 3″ wide by 5″ deep, to form the sides of the dragon's mouth, with a connecting opening across the closed end of the box. Leave the opening big enough to insert the custard cup. Glue rickrack around the mouth for teeth. Glue eyes onto the orange pom-poms, and then glue on top of the head. Cut 2 teardrop-shaped nostrils and a forked tongue from the felt. Glue the nostrils above the mouth and glue the tongue in the open mouth so that it hangs over the lower jaw.

Attach the wings to the back of the head with green plastic tape. To make the body, tape the open ends of the two large boxes together. Tape the head to one end of the body, and tape the open end of the other small box to the other end of the body. Glue a triangle of felt on the closed end of the last box for the tail. Cut circles from red felt and glue them on the body of the dragon for freckles.

Put some pieces of dry ice in a custard cup and place the cup inside the mouth of the dragon. As your party begins, pour hot water over the ice—the hotter the water, the greater the steam. The water will gradually freeze around the dry ice. Remove the cup and run hot water over it periodically to melt the ice from around the dry ice. This process will create more steam. The cup will hold enough dry ice to breathe fire for three to five minutes.

Handling Dry Ice

To find dry ice, look in the yellow pages of your phone book under Ice. Dry ice needs to be handled with caution as its temperature is about 109°F below zero! Don't allow children to handle dry ice and always use gloves to avoid burning your hands. Use a hammer to break large pieces into smaller ones.

PORK AND CABBAGE EGG ROLLS

Egg-roll wrappers are tissue-thin dough, available in the produce section of most supermarkets.

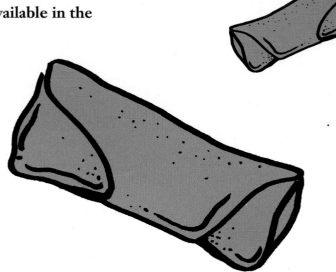

1 pound ground pork, browned
1 small green cabbage, finely chopped (about 3 cups)
1/4 cup minced green onion
1/4 cup minced bamboo shoots
1 tablespoon minced fresh ginger
2 tablespoons soy sauce
1 teaspoon sesame oil
1 teaspoon cornstarch
16–20 square egg-roll wrappers
Oil for frying
Oriental Dipping Sauce

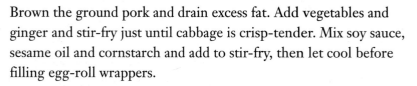

Brown the ground pork and drain excess fat. Add vegetables and ginger and stir-fry just until cabbage is crisp-tender. Mix soy sauce, sesame oil and cornstarch and add to stir-fry, then let cool before filling egg-roll wrappers.

To make the rolls, spread 2 to 3 tablespoons of filling diagonally across the center of a wrapper. Fold one corner over the filling. Moisten with cold water. Fold over the two end corners. Roll the filled portion over to form a package. Press down firmly on the seams to seal the wrappers. Repeat with remaining rolls.

Heat oil in frying pan to 375°F. Fry a few rolls at a time for 3 to 4 minutes, until they are golden brown. Serve hot with plum sauce, hot mustard, soy sauce, or Oriental Dipping Sauce. Serves 4 to 6.

ORIENTAL DIPPING SAUCE

3 tablespoons catsup
1 tablespoon soy sauce
1 teaspoon sugar
1/2 teaspoon minced fresh ginger
1/2 small clove garlic, minced

Combine all ingredients in a small bowl.

> **"When prosperity comes, do not use all of it."**
> —Confucius

Valentine's Day

FEBRUARY 14

The mischievous Cupid from ancient Roman mythology is associated with love and Valentine's Day. Whenever one of Cupid's arrows pierced a person's heart, whomever they were looking at would become their true love!

Everyone knows that Valentine's Day is a special day for love, friendship, sweethearts, pretty cards, and flowers, but no one knows exactly how or why it got started. One legend has it that birds choose their mates on Valentine's Day. Another common myth says that it is celebrated in memory of a Christian martyr named Valentine. He was imprisoned by the Romans in about A.D. 270 because he would not give up his Christian beliefs. Prior to his execution, he wrote a note to the daughter of his jailer and signed it, "Your Valentine." He was later made a saint, and sometimes Valentine's Day is called St. Valentine's Day.

Today it is one of the most widely celebrated unofficial holidays, and a day to let your sweetheart, parents, relatives, and friends know how much you love them.

Nothing conveys love like a handmade gift or treat. The time you spend making these Valentine gifts will show the one you love just how much.

STENCILED HEART QUILT

For those without the time or inclination to appliqué a quilt, this is an easy way to create an heirloom!

*Commercial stencils, stencil paper or
    contact paper*
Glass (from an old picture frame)
X-Acto knife or small, sharp scissors
*Unbleached muslin fabric of desired size,
    prewashed*
Acrylic fabric paints
Stencil brushes

To make your own stencil, draw the design on stencil paper or contact paper. Put a piece of glass under your project and carefully cut the outlines of the design with the knife or scissors. Lift out the portions you'll want to stencil.

Place the stencil on the muslin and carefully hold in place. If using contact paper, peel off the paper backing and carefully smooth the stencil onto the muslin.

Dip the stencil brush into paint and blot. While holding the brush in a vertical position, apply the paint evenly to the exposed areas of the fabric using short strokes. Start each stroke on the stencil and brush paint onto the fabric. Do not add water to the paint or the brush. When all areas are painted, carefully lift off the stencil.

When paint is thoroughly dry, spray the fabric with a mixture of one part white vinegar to one part water. Place an ironing cloth or brown paper bag over the design and press with an iron to "set" the design and make it washable.

Piece strips of contrasting fabric to sides of quilt. Quilt or tie as you would any quilt top.

In the 1850s, a proposal of marriage was frequently made with a Valentine and the suitor was judged by the quality of what he wrote.

BATHROOM TISSUE CATS

Turn a roll of bathroom tissue into a cat or lion for your Valentine.

1 roll bathroom tissue
Black puff paint or magic marker
Red puff paint or cheek blush
Posterboard or cardstock (for ears, paws, and tail)
Sponge
Bow and/or heart-shaped pipe cleaner
Yarn (optional)
Valentine candies
Toothpick

With puff paint or marker, gently sponge or draw a cat or lion face on the tissue roll. Sponge on cheeks with blush or red puff paint, and other facial features with black puff paint or marker. Cut out ears, tail, and paws from posterboard and glue to roll, making sure the paws cover the bottom hole of the tissue roll. Add a bow and heart-shaped pipe cleaner. Decorate with yarn "fur" if desired. Fill the roll's center with candy hearts, kisses, or other small Valentine candies. Glue a foil or paper heart with a love message ("You're Purr-fect" or "No Lion—I Love You") to a toothpick and push into the top of the roll.

PHOTO VALENTINE

Make one each year and your child's grandparents will have a collection of special Valentines to save and compare.

Red construction paper or posterboard
Decorations—lace, puff paint, etc.
Glue
Child's picture

Make a heart out of red construction paper or posterboard, and cut a circle or smaller heart shape from the middle. (You may want to use newspaper to cut out a pattern first.) Have the child decorate the Valentine for their grandparents by gluing lace around the outer edge, drawing hearts or Cupids, and writing a message with puff paint. Glue the child's picture on the back side so that it shows through the smaller heart cutout.

Another idea is to decorate a large red heart with a hole in the center, large enough for the child's face to show through. Take a picture and send to grandparents.

The word *lace* comes from the Latin word *laqueus*, which means "a snare or noose." Perhaps you'll snare your lover's heart when you send a Valentine decorated with lace!

HEART-SHAPED CUPCAKES

It's easy to make heart-shaped cupcakes using your favorite recipe!

Cake batter
Paper baking cups
Marbles or aluminum foil

Line muffin pans with paper baking cups and fill 1/2 full with batter. Place a marble or small ball of aluminum foil in each cup between the paper liner and the pan to make the heart-shaped mold. If the cups aren't about 2/3 full, add a little more batter. Don't overfill the cups or you'll lose the heart shape. Bake as usual. Frost the cupcakes, pipe decorative frosting around the outside to further define the heart shape, and decorate with Valentine candies.

VALENTINE LEI

Give your love this Hawaiian Valentine.

Plastic wrap
Small Valentine cookies or candies
Red or pink ribbon

Tear off a sheet of plastic wrap as long as you want your lei/necklace to be, plus 6″. Place candy/cookies face down and centered across the wrap, leaving an extra 3″ at each end. Fold top portion of wrap over sweets, then the bottom portion up. Scrunch wrap between pieces and tie with ribbon so that you have alternating goodies and bows. Knot both ends. Secure ends around neck with ribbon.

Heart-Shaped Edibles

Use a heart-shaped cookie cutter to cut hearts from foods such as biscuit dough or jelled gelatin. Place an open-topped, heart-shaped cookie cutter on the griddle and pour pancake batter into the cutter (or you can just try to pour the batter in a heart shape). Trim slices of bread into hearts for special Valentine sandwiches.

HEART CAKE

Make a heart-shaped cake without purchasing a special pan.

1 cake mix
1 9" round cake pan
1 9" square baking pan
1 recipe white frosting
Cherry pie filling

Make cake batter according to package directions and pour into greased and floured cake pans. Bake as directed. Cool cake 10 minutes in pan on cooling rack. Remove from pans.

Place the square cake diamond fashion on the serving dish. Cut the round cake in half and place each half with cut side next to a square side to form a heart. Frost with white icing and make a border around the outer edge to hold the filling. Top with cherry pie filling.

SUPER KISS

Give someone special a super kiss.

1 cube butter or margarine
1 (16 ounce) package miniature marshmallows
12 cups regular or chocolate crispy rice cereal
Large plastic funnels, buttered (Tupperware is best)
Cookie sheet
Plastic wrap
Ribbon

Melt butter or margarine in large saucepan over low to medium heat. Add marshmallows and cook until marshmallows are completely melted, stirring constantly. Remove from heat and add cereal; stir until well coated. Cool slightly, but not completely. Butter your fingers and press warm mixture into buttered plastic funnels and place on a cookie sheet. When cool, unmold and wrap in plastic. Add a flag with a Valentine message taped to a toothpick. Makes 2 to 4 large kisses.

DINOSAUR

You Are Dino-mite!

1 pink Hostess SnoBall snack cake
3 candy corns
8 gumdrops
Toothpicks
Licorice (mouth)

Use the snack cake for the body and push candy
corns into the top to form the dinosaur's spine.
Use toothpicks to attach licorice and gumdrop pieces for eyes, cheeks, and feet.

DING DONG DRUM

My Heart Beats for You!

1 Hostess Ding Dong snack cake
White frosting
2 pretzel sticks
2 gumdrops

Pipe large connecting "X's" of frosting around the snack cake. Use two
pretzel sticks with a gumdrop stuck on one end for the drumsticks.

FRIENDLY CLOWN

Quit Clowning Around! Be My Friend!

1 pink or white Hostess SnoBall snack cake
1 black gumdrop
Purple candies
1 large red gumdrop
3" piece of red string licorice
Toasted coconut
1 sugar cone
Surprise gift inside hat (candy, toy, or jewelry)
Heart candies
1 large pink gumdrop
Decorating icing

Use the snack cake for the clown's head. Attach
facial features and hair with decorating icing. Make the face by cutting the black
gumdrop in half vertically for the eyes and adding purple candies to make irises. The
nose is a large red gumdrop, and the mouth is a string of red licorice. Top with
toasted coconut hair. Fill the sugar cone with a surprise gift and invert for a hat.
Decorate the hat with heart candies and top with a large pink gumdrop.

A SQUEEZE AND A KISS

If you can't give your sweetheart a squeeze and a kiss in person, send this!

1 squeeze-it container of Kool-Aid
1 Hershey's Kiss

Hang a note around the container that reads "Here's a squeeze and a kiss" but use a Hershey's Kiss instead of the word.

SNOW BUNNY

Every Bunny Needs Some Bunny to Love.

1 white Hostess SnoBall snack cake
2 small black gumdrops
1 small red gumdrop
Toothpicks
Red string licorice
Pink posterboard or construction paper

Attach small black gumdrop eyes and a small red gumdrop nose to the snack cake with toothpick halves. For the mouth and whiskers, use red string licorice. Cut two ears from pink posterboard or construction paper and push into the top of the bunny head.

SNOW KITTEN

You're Purr-fect for Me!

1 white Hostess SnoBall snack cake
3 heart-shaped candies
Red string licorice
Toothpicks
Strawberry fruit roll (or pink posterboard or construction paper)

Use the snack cake as the head, and attach heart-shaped candies for the eyes and nose. Use red string licorice for the mouth and whiskers. The small, triangular cat's ears are cut from a fruit roll (or posterboard or construction paper).

GIANT COOKIE HEART

Be big-hearted on Valentine's Day and make an oversize cookie heart.

1 recipe sugar cookie dough
Heart-shaped cake pan or pattern

Grease a baking sheet. Roll sugar cookie dough, and cut in heart shape or pat dough into a heart-shaped pan. (To lift the giant cookie onto the baking sheet without tearing, roll the cookie around the rolling pin, carefully lift, and unroll it onto the baking sheet.) Bake in 375°F preheated oven for 10 to 12 minutes. Allow to cool completely. Frost and decorate as desired.

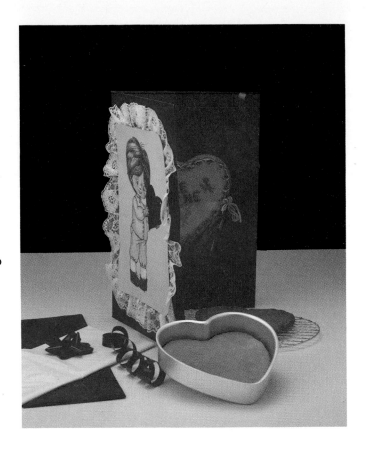

VALENTINE MERINGUE

This delicate dessert will capture anyone's heart.

Aluminum foil or heavy brown paper
1/2 cup egg whites (whites of about 4 large eggs) at
*   room temperature*
1/4 teaspoon cream of tartar
Dash salt
1 cup sugar
1 teaspoon vanilla extract
A few drops red food coloring (optional)
1 quart strawberry ice cream
1 (8 ounce) jar strawberry topping

Preheat oven to 225°F. Cut aluminum foil or heavy brown paper to fit cookie sheet. In glass or stainless steel bowl, beat egg whites, cream of tartar, and salt until foamy. Gradually add sugar, one tablespoon at a time, beating after each addition, and continue beating until meringue holds a stiff peak. Fold in vanilla and add food coloring, if desired. Spoon meringue in heart shapes onto baking sheet, or form in hearts using pastry bag with large tip. Make a depression in the center with the back of a spoon. Bake for 40 to 60 minutes or until lightly browned. Remove from cookie sheet. Fill shell with strawberry ice cream and top with strawberry topping. Serves 6 to 8.

Presidents' Day

Presidents' Day honors the contributions of two of our greatest and best-loved presidents, George Washington, born on February 22, 1732, and Abraham Lincoln, born on February 12, 1809, nine years after Washington's death.

George Washington is one of the most honored men in U.S. history. He was the commander in chief of the first American army, and after the revolution was elected to be our first president. Following the precedent of honoring English kings, many Americans celebrated Washington's birth during his lifetime. In the winter of 1778, the Fourth Continental Artillery band marched to Valley Forge and serenaded him on his birthday. The University of Pennsylvania has held regular exercises in honor of Washington's birthday longer than any other institution. Faculty members marched to the President's house in Philadelphia on his birthday in 1794.

Not long after Washington's death in 1799, Congress passed a resolution that February 22, 1800, should be observed as a day of mourning. Over the years, this became a tradition throughout the nation.

The late Arthur M. Schlesinger, Sr., a Harvard professor, requested that 55 historians rank the Presidents in order of greatness. They chose Lincoln, Washington, Franklin D. Roosevelt, Wilson, Jefferson, and Jackson, in that order. Lincoln's rise from a log cabin to the presidency, his shrewd insight, humility, and story-telling genius, as well as his assassination, have all added to

John F. Kennedy's Tribute to Washington

"As time goes on, we realize more and more how deep is our debt to George Washington, and his strict sense of sacrifice and duty to his country. We are ever mindful of all he gave of himself in order that this country, in its infancy, might survive, grow, and prosper.

"As in the past, this anniversary of the birth of the father of our country inspires us anew with the strength for today's challenges.

"The spirit of George Washington is a living tradition, so that even today he serves his country well."

the love and devotion Americans feel for him. During his presidency, Lincoln fought to preserve the Union, and the Emancipation Proclamation was his most far-reaching action. Only five days after the Confederate surrender, he was shot by John Wilkes Booth while attending the theatre, and he died the next morning, April 15, 1865.

The first formal observance of Lincoln's birthday was held in the Capitol building in Washington on February 12, 1866. As is the case with several of our holidays, the centennial of Lincoln's Birthday on February 12, 1909, provided the impetus for Congress to firmly establish the holiday.

When the Monday Holiday Law was passed, the observation of both birthdays was combined into Presidents' Day. Washington and Lincoln both cared deeply about the ideals upon which their country was founded and they gave their talents and energies to upholding those ideals.

Abraham Lincoln

Lincoln stood 6′4″ and towered over most other men of his day. He was thin and awkward, but made friends easily and loved to tell jokes. With only a year of formal schooling, his education came from his love of reading. "The books, and your capacity for understanding them, are just the same in all places. . . . Always bear in mind that your own resolution to succeed is more important than any other one thing."

One of Lincoln's greatest assets was his ability to express his convictions clearly and with great force. Many people consider him the most eloquent speechmaker of any American president. It is almost impossible to repeat his words aloud without feeling their power and the fervent beliefs they represent. Lincoln would be surprised to find that many of his speeches are now considered great literature. "I do the very best I know how—the very best I can; and I mean to keep on doing so."

Lincoln's birth in a tiny log cabin and the story (probably fictional) of Washington and the cherry tree are well known in American folklore. A Lincoln Log Cake, Washington Cherry Tarts, and a Lincoln Log Cabin are fun ways to remember these two great leaders!

LINCOLN LOG CAKE

Really great with ice cream!

1 chocolate cake mix, prepared according to directions
1 (16 ounce) can milk chocolate frosting
1 (16 ounce) can dark chocolate frosting
Pastry bag
3/8" or 1/2" round pastry tip
Maraschino cherries with stems attached
Paper hatchet

Preheat oven to 375°F. Grease a 15" x 10" baking pan and line with waxed paper. Grease waxed paper. Gently spread prepared cake batter in pan. Bake 10 to 12 minutes. Sprinkle powdered sugar on a clean, dry dish towel. When cake is done, loosen edges and immediately invert on prepared towel. Remove pan and wax paper. Starting with longer edge of cake, roll up cake and towel together. Cool. Unroll cake and remove towel. Reroll cake without towel and frost with milk chocolate frosting, swirling with a spatula to resemble bark.

Fill the pastry bag with dark chocolate frosting. To create a log effect, make horizontal lines the length of the cake and rings on each end. Top with 3 maraschino cherries (with stems) and place a miniature paper hatchet into the log.

Note: Cake can be filled with a chocolate buttercream filling, softened ice cream, or another filling of your choice. Roll the cake with the towel and cool. Unroll, remove the towel, spread the cake with filling, then reroll, frost, and decorate. (Store an ice cream cake in the freezer.)

WASHINGTON CHERRY TARTS

Super quick and easy, and the hatchet makes it special.

Piecrust dough
Tart-sized foil pans
1 can cherry pie filling

Cut small circular pie shells to fit the tart pans and prick the shells with a fork. Draw a hatchet on heavy paper to use as a pattern and cut a hatchet for each tart from the remaining piecrust. Bake crusts and hatchets according to recipe or box directions. Fill crusts with cherry pie filling and place a hatchet on top of each tart.

LINCOLN LOG CABIN

This log cabin can be completely landscaped, including a meadow, duck pond, and wishing well.

12 (10") hard breadsticks
18 (6") hard breadsticks
Processed cheese spread (in a pressure can)
3 slices Cheddar cheese
2 pieces (8-1/2" x 11") brown or tan cardstock
Styrofoam base (12" x 24"; 2" thick)
Heavy-duty aluminum foil
2 or 3 heads Romaine lettuce
2 (1/4 ounce) envelopes unflavored gelatin
1 (3 ounce) package blueberry flavored gelatin
1 cup boiling water
6" pie tin or small dish
Nonstick cooking spray
Duck-shaped crackers
1 red bell pepper
Round toothpicks
Small quantities of vegetables: celery, cucumber, carrot, cauliflower,
*   radishes, and broccoli*
3 wooden skewers

In 1861, President Abraham Lincoln said, "The Declaration of Independence gave liberty not alone to the people of this country, but hope to all of the world for all future time."

Construct the cabin the way you would build a house from toy Lincoln Logs, using 10" breadsticks for the long side and 6" breadsticks for the short side, with processed cheese as glue to hold the breadsticks together. (If you're not planning to eat your log cabin, you can apply glue with a glue gun instead of cheese.) Lay two 10" breadsticks parallel to each other, about 4-1/2" apart. Squirt cheese about 1/2" from each end of the two breadsticks. Lay 6" breadsticks on the cheese, at right angles to the 10" sticks, to complete the rectangle. Squirt cheese 1/2" from each end of the 6" breadsticks and repeat the process until your cabin is 5 to 6 breadsticks high on each side.

Cut rectangular windows and a door from the Cheddar cheese slices and fasten them in appropriate places on one long side of the cabin using the pressurized cheese. Fold one piece of cardstock in half vertically to form the roof and secure with more cheese.

Cover the Styrofoam with foil. Overlap lettuce leaves to make it look like a grass-covered meadow, working from the center to the edge of the foil-covered Styrofoam. Place the cabin on the base.

Spray a small pie tin or shallow dish with nonstick cooking spray. Dissolve all three packages of gelatin in 1 cup of boiling water. Pour into the dish and refrigerate. When the gelatin has set, slip it from the mold, nesting it between lettuce leaves. Add cracker ducks swimming on the pond.

Make a wishing well by cutting the top from the bell pepper. Clean out any seeds and membrane. Secure the bell pepper to the base with toothpicks. Cut one 6″ breadstick in half. Use two pieces of toothpick to fasten the two halves to the bell pepper to form supports for the roof. Another toothpick placed horizontally between the breadstick pieces forms a crosspiece. Press the breadsticks against the sharp ends of the toothpick to secure them. Cut a 4″ square from cardstock, then fold it in half and glue with cheese to finish the roof of the wishing well.

Fasten two 4″–5″ celery sticks together with cheese to form the barrel of a cannon. Secure two cucumber slices to the cannon sides with toothpicks for wheels.

Fasten thin carrot slices to the Styrofoam with toothpick pieces to form paths. Cauliflower pieces, radishes cut as flowers, and short broccoli stalks fastened upright on the Styrofoam with toothpicks make shrubs and small trees to surround your cabin and wishing well. Fasten larger stalks of broccoli to the Styrofoam with bamboo or wooden skewers for mature trees.

Break up remaining breadsticks to make a woodpile at the side of the cabin.

Leap Year Day

FEBRUARY 29 (EVERY FOURTH YEAR)

In most years, February has 28 days, but if the year is divisible by four and not divisible by four hundred, February has 29 days. The earth takes 365 days, 5 hours, 48 minutes, and about 46 seconds to travel around the sun, so every four years one extra day is added to February to even things out.

The year with the extra day may have been called leap year by the English because after February 29, a date "leaps over" a day of the week. February 29th also had no legal status in English courts, and was "leapt over" as far as the records were concerned. Everything that happened on February 29 was dated as occurring on February 28.

People have traditionally done things on Leap Year Day that they wouldn't normally do. For instance, on Leap Year Day a woman could propose marriage, when that wasn't normally acceptable. Scotland, France, Switzerland, and other countries even passed laws giving a woman the prerogative to propose, and imposing penalties that the man had to pay if he refused. One legend traces the origins of this custom to St. Patrick and St. Bridget in Ireland.

Start thinking now of outrageous, weird and backward things to do once every four years. This is a day to have fun and let your imagination run wild!

Inside-Out-and-Backward Ideas

- Wear your clothes inside out or backward
- Check with the principal to see if school classes can be held in reverse order
- Eat dinner in the morning and breakfast in the evening
- Eat dessert before the main meal
- Have a backward spelling bee and spell the words backward
- Have a backward relay race, starting at the finish line
- Reverse family roles and jobs for the day
- Have a girl-ask-guy party or dance

If you were born on Leap Year Day, you would only get a birthday every four years. You would only have four birthdays by the time you're old enough to vote!

MARCH

Whether March comes in like a lion or a lamb, it's the last long wait for spring to begin. Although Easter occasionally comes in March, there's usually only one major holiday—St. Patrick's Day. But what a holiday! There are so many opportunities to enjoy the green while waiting for the green of the new season. Parades and festivities bring family and friends together.

St. Patrick's Day is the traditional day to turn stock out to pasture for the summer and plant potatoes. Potatoes have been an important food in Ireland for hundreds of years. From 1845 to 1847, Ireland's potato crop failed because of a plant disease, and about 750,000 people died of starvation or disease.

Potatoes grow well in Ireland's climate and are used in a wide variety of dishes. Try some Irish Potato Skins on St. Patrick's Day, or anytime you need a delicious appetizer or main dish.

Everyone in your family will delight in a day of green edibles. You'll be surprised at how many green foods there are! It's a day to have fun with food, whether with your family or guests. Start the day with green Shamrock Pancakes and a glass of Magic Green Milk, and try some savory Pesto Pasta for dinner.

If the March winds aren't blowing *too* hard, hang a Leprechaun Wind Sock on your front porch. The Rainbow and Pot of Gold Centerpiece will bring a little "luck o' the Irish" into your household.

St. Patrick's Day

MARCH 17

This holiday honors Saint Patrick, the patron saint of Ireland, and is celebrated by Americans of Irish descent and many other nationalities with parades, dinners, Irish jigs, and songs. There are more people of Irish descent in the United States than there are in Ireland!

Saint Patrick spent most of his life teaching the people of Ireland to read and write while converting them to Christianity. He tried to combine old customs with new meanings. As time went on, he was loved more and more, and when he died, all of Ireland went into mourning. Thousands of mourners came to his funeral from long distances, carrying so many candles and torches that it is said that everything was as light as day. The sun refused to set for 12 days and nights, but stood perfectly still so as not to bring a new day without him. St. Patrick's Day commemorates the anniversary of his death in A.D. 461.

As the Roman Empire collapsed and Europe was overrun by barbarians, Saint Patrick's teachings kept learning alive in Ireland, and Ireland became known as the "Island of Saints and Scholars." Saint Patrick is credited with almost single-handedly preserving the fundamentals of civilization for the Western world, and it is through him that Ireland has its centuries-old tradition of scholarship and literature.

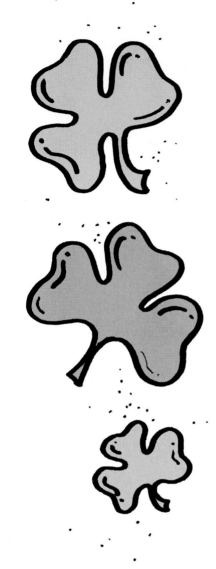

Ireland is known as the *Emerald Isle* because of the lush green color of the landscape. Its mild, moist climate is ideal for vegetation, and a type of clover called *shamrock* grows everywhere. This three-leafed plant has become a symbol of Irish heritage, and many people wear green sprigs of shamrock on St. Patrick's Day.

Don't be shy about having fun with green on St. Patrick's Day. These food and decorating ideas are fun, especially for children.

LEPRECHAUN CENTERPIECE

Sure to delight even the littlest elf in your family.

Dimensional craft paint
Tangerine
Green and flesh-colored felt
Glue
Green apple
Toothpicks
Orange chenille trim, fringe trim or yarn
for beard
Small black felt doll's hat (available from
craft stores)
1/2 yard (1/2" wide) green ribbon

Paint eyes and mouth on tangerine. Cut a 1″ by 5″ strip from the green felt for the arms, adjusting the length to fit your apple. Cut hands from flesh-colored felt and glue a hand to the end of each arm. Turn the apple upside down. Place the arm-strip across apple, and insert a toothpick through the felt and partway into the blossom end of the apple. Place the tangerine on the other end of the toothpick for the head. Attach trim or yarn with glue or pins to form a beard. Decorate hatband with ribbon and place hat on top of tangerine. Keep in place with straight pins. Tie ribbon into bow and place on neck.

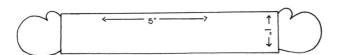

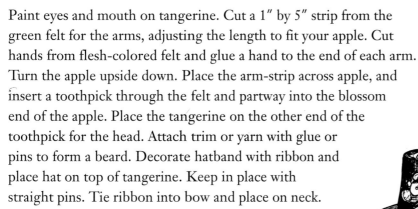

Leprechauns are small imaginary creatures who supposedly made shoes for the fairies of Ireland. These little old men have a reputation for being rich and quite cranky. If captured, a leprechaun will try to buy his freedom by telling his captor where to find the pot of gold that he's hidden.

LEPRECHAUN WIND SOCK

Hang this on your porch or suspend it from your dining room light fixture on St. Patrick's Day.

5" x 3" flesh-colored fun foam (face & hands)
6" x 12" green fun foam (body)
2" x 12" black fun foam (hat & shoes)
Scissors
1 small pink pom-pom (nose)
Wiggly eyes (or cut round pieces of black fun foam)
Red or pink permanent marker
Orange chenille trim (beard)
1 yard (1-1/2" wide) St. Patrick's ribbon
Craft glue
1-1/2 yards (3/8" wide) gold metallic ribbon
3 buttons
2 yards (1/8" wide) ribbon
(Note: Fun foam is available at craft stores in 11-1/2" x 17-1/2" sheets.)

For the head, cut a 3-1/2" wide by 2-1/2" long strip of flesh-colored fun foam, and round the bottom corners to form the jaw. Cut notches at top corners to form ears. Center head on one 12" side of the green fun foam, so that the top of the head is even with the top of the green body, and glue in place. Glue the pom-pom nose and eyes onto the face. Draw mouth and cheeks with permanent marker. Glue beard trim around the face.

Cut hat out of a 4-1/2" x 2" piece of black fun foam and cut shoes out of 2" x 3" pieces of black fun foam. Cut hands out of 1-1/2" x 1-1/2" pieces of flesh fun foam. Glue hat on top of head, so that the ears stick out. Glue hands to 6-1/2" lengths of 1-1/2" wide ribbon, and trim the top ends of the ribbons to form rounded shoulders. Glue feet to 11" lengths of ribbon. Glue tops of ribbon *shoulders* just to the sides of the jawline, approximately 1-1/2" from the top of the green body. Glue ribbon legs to the bottom of the body, on the back side of the foam, about 1" apart.

Roll sides of body back into a cylinder and glue closed. Decorate with a bow tie and a hatband made of narrow gold ribbon, and three buttons down the front. To hang, punch holes on the top sides of the body and tie 1 yard of narrow ribbon to each side.

RAINBOW AND POT OF GOLD CENTERPIECE

This centerpiece doubles as your fruit salad!

Styrofoam wreath form (24" diameter), cut in half
Aluminum foil
Leaf lettuce
Rainbow-colored fruits: apple halves, strawberries, orange slices, pineapple, grapes, and blueberries
Toothpicks
Gold foil-covered chocolate coins
Small pot, dry ice, and warm water

Completely cover one Styrofoam half with aluminum foil. Using toothpicks, cover the bottom of the Styrofoam with leaf lettuce. Attach fruit in rows to resemble a rainbow (red, orange, yellow, green, blue, violet), completely covering the Styrofoam.

Place one end of the rainbow next to a pot filled with dry ice. Spread coins around the pot and under the rainbow. Pour a little warm water over dry ice and watch the steam.

Dip cut apples in lemon juice or ascorbic acid to keep them from turning brown.

SHAMROCK BREAD LOAF

Green, but not moldy!

2 packages active dry yeast

1-1/4 cups warm water
(105° to 115°F)

Green food coloring

1 cup warm water

3 tablespoons sugar

2 teaspoons salt

3 tablespoons shortening

6 to 6-1/2 cups bread flour

Butter, softened

2 (1" x 14") strips of brown paper or parchment baking
paper, well buttered (do not use recycled grocery bags)

Florist pins, straight pins, or T-pins

1" wide green ribbon

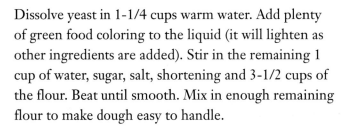

Dissolve yeast in 1-1/4 cups warm water. Add plenty of green food coloring to the liquid (it will lighten as other ingredients are added). Stir in the remaining 1 cup of water, sugar, salt, shortening and 3-1/2 cups of the flour. Beat until smooth. Mix in enough remaining flour to make dough easy to handle.

Turn dough onto lightly floured surface. Knead until smooth and elastic, about 10 minutes. Place in greased bowl; turn greased side up. Cover; let rise in warm place until double, about 1 hour. Dough is ready if indentation remains when touched.

Punch down dough and divide into halves. Let rest 10 minutes. Shape each half into a smooth, round ball. Brush lightly with butter.

To make depressions for the ribbon, tie each loaf with 1" wide heavy brown paper strips, creating four quarters. Fasten with a pin. Place each loaf on a 12" x 18" greased baking sheet or a 12"–14" pizza pan.

Let rise until double, about 1 hour. Heat oven to 350°F. Bake loaves on center rack 35 to 40 minutes until golden. Immediately remove from pans. Brush tops with butter; cool on wire racks. After bread has cooled, remove paper strips and replace with green ribbon and a bow.

Green Food Surprises for St. Patrick's Day

♣ *Magic Green Milk*

Pour 2 to 3 drops of green food coloring in clear milk glasses. When the children come in to eat, pour milk in the glasses. The milk will swirl green—like magic!

♣ *Shamrock Pancakes*

Add green food coloring to your pancake batter and cook in the shape of shamrocks.

♣ *Green Potatoes*

Blend green food coloring with the milk for mashed potatoes.

♣ *Shamrock Pizza*

Shape a shamrock on a large pizza pan or baking sheet with three circular pizzas and one thin, rectangular one for the stem. Mix equal amounts of green food coloring and water and brush on outer edges of crust. Shake grated cheese with remaining food coloring mixture in a closed plastic bag or container. Top with family favorites (each leaf can be different) and bake as usual.

PESTO PASTA

Go ahead and use your hands to mix the pesto and pasta.

1 pound spinach pasta (angel hair is a good choice)
1 teaspoon salt (optional)
1 tablespoon light olive oil
1 or 2 cloves garlic
2 cups lightly packed fresh basil leaves
1/2 cup light olive oil
3 tablespoons slivered almonds
1 cup (about 5 ounces) grated Parmesan cheese
2 tablespoons dried tomatoes, chopped (or fresh tomatoes)

Cook the pasta according to package directions, adding salt and 1 tablespoon of olive oil to the water. When cooked, rinse in cold water and set aside.

Chop garlic in a blender or food processor. Add basil and 1/2 cup of olive oil, and process until basil leaves are finely chopped. Add almonds and pulse. Add cheese and pulse.

In a large bowl, toss pasta, pesto, and tomatoes. Serve cold or heat in microwave on low. Serves 4 to 6.

AN IRISH BLESSING

May the road rise to meet you;
May the wind be always at your back;
May the sun shine warm upon your face;
May the rains fall soft upon your fields;
And until we meet again,
May God hold you in the hollow of his hand.

Gala Green Fruits and Veggies

There are lots of green fruits and vegetables you can add to your green dinner table. Look around the grocery store for green fruits, including apples, kiwi, green grapes, honeydew melon, Bartlett pears, and limes. Green veggies are plentiful, too. You can pick from asparagus, avocados, green beans, lima beans, broccoli, Brussels sprouts, cabbage, celery, collard greens, cucumbers, kale, lettuce, okra, green olives, green onions, green peppers, parsley, peas, spinach, Swiss chard, and zucchini. You could also serve spinach dip or spinach pasta with green pesto. Open your mind and turn your imagination loose as you stroll the aisles in preparation for St. Patrick's Day.

IRISH POTATO SKINS

Serve as an appetizer or as a main dish with a crisp green salad.

4 large baking potatoes
2 tablespoons butter, melted
Seasoned salt
Pepper

POTATO SKIN TOPPINGS

1-1/2 cups (6 ounces) grated Cheddar cheese
1/3 cup chopped green onions (5–6 onions)
6 crisp-cooked bacon slices, crumbled
1/4 cup low-fat sour cream
1 (5-3/4 ounce) can black olives, chopped
1 green pepper, finely chopped
1 tomato, finely chopped

Preheat oven to 400°F. Scrub and dry potatoes; prick with a fork. Bake 50 to 60 minutes or until soft. Cool enough to handle. Cut each potato in half lengthwise. Scoop out pulp with a spoon, leaving about 1/2″ of potato in the shell. Set potato pulp aside for potato salad or hash browns. Place potato shells, skin-side down, in a 13″ x 9″ baking pan. Brush inside of shells with melted butter. Sprinkle with seasoned salt and pepper. Bake 10–15 minutes until golden and serve hot. If you prefer, potato halves can be cut in bite-sized pieces. Let each person garnish with favorite toppings. Serves 4 to 6.

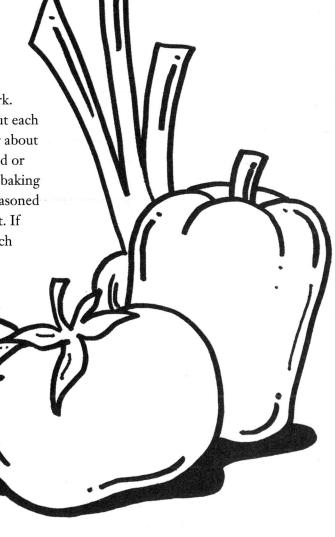

APRIL

Ah, it's spring at last! The days begin to last longer than the nights after the spring equinox on March 21. Spring is the season for new beginnings, and nature is full of energy for growth and new life. Take a walk in the park or just stroll around the block to see all the beauty spring brings.

You'll find many wonderful ways to celebrate Easter in this chapter. You can make an Easter tree with hatching chick and bunny ornaments, a chocolate Easter basket with lots of surprises inside, and Easter egg animals. Try growing your own Easter basket with real grass!

It wouldn't be Easter without bunnies. Make an adorable bunny cake that will delight the kids. It's fun and very easy to put together. There are also lots of ways to use all those leftover Easter eggs.

While Easter may be the focus of the month, start April with some wonderful April Fool's Day tricks that will surprise and delight your family and friends.

Don't forget Earth Day on the 22nd. It's the day to renew your commitment to recycling, use environmentally friendly household products, and do your part in taking care of our planet.

Celebrate Arbor Day on the last Friday in April. It's a thoughtful day to plant a new tree or build a birdhouse for the feathered friends in your yard.

April Fool's Day

No one is quite sure how April Fool's Day began. Some think it started with the spring equinox celebration. Others trace it to France when Charles IV in 1564 adopted the Gregorian calendar that changed the new year from April 1 to January 1. Since news traveled slowly in those days, many French citizens continued to observe the new year in the spring, making New Year's Day calls and sending presents to friends and relatives. The day gradually evolved into a joke, and mock gifts were sent on the first of April. As time passed, it was customary for the French to pull all kinds of practical jokes on April 1.

The custom spread from France to the British Isles where it became a day for wild pranks. People were frequently sent on bizarre errands that sometimes required journeys of several days. The early settlers from England brought the hilarity of April Fool's Day with them to the New World.

Your family and friends will wonder where all this silliness comes from when you pull some of these foolers on them.

SNAKE SHIRT

Children will have great fun fooling someone with this snake tie-dyed shirt!

Light-colored T-shirt
1 yard (22-gauge) wire
5 yards colored string
Needle and thread
3"– 4" length (1/4") red ribbon (mouth)
2 buttons (eyes)
Fabric dyes (red, yellow, and green)
Small brush or sponge
Vinegar

Place the wire diagonally across the shirt, from shoulder to hip. Fold the shirt over the wire and then roll it up. Tie the string around the shirt 2" from one end and wrap tightly to the other end of the shirt. Wrap the string back up the snake a few inches and tie off.

With needle and thread, fashion a head from the shoulder end of the shirt, tacking the ribbon in place for the mouth and buttons for eyes. Use fabric dyes to paint the back of the snake.

After you've surprised your best friend with your tie-dyed snake, remove the string. Spray with vinegar and iron the fabric paint with a hot iron to set the colors.

GLUE A PENNY TO A SIDEWALK

See a penny, pick it up. All the day, you'll have good luck, but only if the head is up.

Tempt your friends and family by gluing a shiny new penny head-side up on the sidewalk or front stoop. Sit back and watch how many people try to grab some luck.

JOKE TAPE

You'll keep your listener chuckling all year with this "gag gift."

Check out a joke book from the library and record your favorite jokes on tape. Pause for a couple of seconds after each joke to give time for laughter! You could also record riddles, but record the answers on another tape and hide it. Put clues on the first tape to help them find the answer tape.

BACKWARD WRITING

Write a secret message that can only be read in the mirror!

Using a dark-colored marker, write a message on a light-colored, lightweight piece of paper. Flip the paper over and put another light-colored, lightweight piece of paper on top, and copy the message backward. See if your friend can figure out how to read it.

INVISIBLE WRITING

Young children will be delighted with this fun activity.

Dip a cotton swab in milk or lemon juice and use it to write a message on a piece of paper. Send it to a friend with instructions to iron the paper to read the hidden message. Like magic, the message will appear in light-brown writing.

SPAGHETTI TOSS

Pig out on Pighetti! Your children and friends won't believe (or forget) this dinner.

1 towel for each guest
2 clothespins for each guest
New plastic tablecloth
Kitchen utensils
Spaghetti and sauce
Garlic bread
Green salad

Before you begin, provide each guest with a bib made from a towel and two clothespins. Cover the table with a **new, clean**, plastic tablecloth that can be thrown away after dinner. Dig out all of your kitchen utensils, such as ice cream scoops, tongs, wire whips, and spatulas. Have each guest choose an "eating" utensil. (No forks or spoons allowed!)

Cook a batch of spaghetti and sauce appropriate for the number of guests you're serving. Dump the spaghetti and sauce in the middle of the table and tell everyone to dig in. Plop a serving of salad and garlic bread next to each guest.

Easter Sunday

Easter Sunday is the Christian festival honoring Christ's resurrection and is considered by many people the world over to be the most important religious observance. It is a day of rejoicing for all Christian faiths.

The word Easter first came into use in A.D. 735. Eostre, or Eastre, was the Teutonic goddess, the deity of both the dawn and spring. The word was transferred to the holiday we now celebrate when the Saxons began to commemorate Christ's resurrection. Easter falls on the first Sunday following the first full moon after the spring equinox.

Constantine the Great ordered the court to wear their finest garments on Easter, which may have been the beginnings of the Easter parade. Even today, it is customary to have a new outfit and bonnet to wear to church on Easter Sunday.

New clothes, Easter bunnies, chicks, lilies, and other Easter trappings are all symbols of the real meaning of Easter, the resurrection and life everlasting. A sunrise service, frequently held out-of-doors, is the highlight of the year in many churches.

Eggs are associated with Easter and are symbols of the resurrection. Eggs hold the seeds of life and represent fertility. Coloring eggs goes back to ancient times when eggs were dyed for spring festivals. Eggs in medieval times were dyed red in memory of the blood that Christ shed. In many European countries, egg decorating is a fine art, especially in Russia and the Ukraine. Several days are spent decorating just one egg.

Folklore has it that an Easter egg with two yolks is a sign of coming financial prosperity, and refusing the gift of an Easter egg endangers your friendship with the giver. In China today, a brilliant red egg is sent as a sign of happiness to friends and relatives when a child is born.

The Easter rabbit tradition originated in Germany. Since rabbits are so prolific, they are said to be symbols of fertility. Tales were told that the Easter bunny laid the eggs for which the children searched in the grass.

The way you choose to celebrate Easter is a personal choice. Along with the new clothes and fun Easter crafts, it would be nice to share with your family the origins of the symbolism we now associate with this holiday. For Christians, attending the church of your choice, perhaps a sunrise service, will reinforce the true meaning of Easter.

Easter is also a wonderful holiday to celebrate the renewal the spring season brings and to show your creative side. These basket crafts and goodies will make Easter a fun and memorable time for your family.

Easter egg hunts are common in parks and private homes across the nation on Easter Sunday. Often the child who finds the most eggs receives a prize, perhaps an Easter basket filled with chocolate eggs, candy chicks, marshmallow bunnies, and cellophane Easter grass.

STRING BASKET

You can also fill this basket with hollow decorated eggs.

1 cup sugar
1 cup hot water
1 rounded, tear-shaped balloon
Crochet-cotton string (available at fabric or craft stores)
Bows, ribbons, and other trims
Easter grass and candies

Make a solution of sugar and hot water, and stir until sugar is dissolved. While the solution is cooling, blow up the balloon and tie the end securely. Tie one end of the string to the knot in the balloon and wrap the string around the balloon in criss-crossing patterns. Pour the sugar solution in a large bowl and rotate the balloon until the string is completely saturated. Hang the balloon over a sink or bathtub to catch the sticky drips as it dries.

When the string is completely dry (about 24 hours), pop the balloon with a straight pin and carefully detach the string from the balloon. Cut the string to form the top edge and handle of the basket, and trim the cut edges with ribbon. Add a decorative bow and fill with Easter grass, lightweight decorations, and candies.

PAPER BAG BUNNY BASKET

This bunny basket is so simple, even preschoolers can make it.

1 (lunch-size) paper bag
Pencil
Scissors
1 small pink pom-pom
Magic marker
Pipe cleaners
Cotton ball
1 (1/2 gallon) milk carton, washed
Easter grass and candies

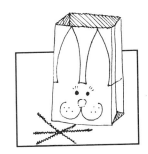

Lay the paper bag flat with the glued side down. Sketch a pair of rabbit ears on the top half of the bag. Cut the ears out, leaving the front and back ears attached to the bag. Cut the sides of the bag even with the bottom of the ears and cut the milk carton to the same height. Decorate the bag with a bunny face and finish with a small pink pom-pom nose, pipe-cleaner whiskers, and a cotton-ball tail. Insert the milk carton in the bag and fill with Easter grass and candies. Glue the front and back ears together at the very tops.

TISSUE EASTER BASKETS

Use paper towels to make larger bunnies, ducks, and chicks.

1 roll bathroom tissue for each basket
Magic markers (to draw faces)
Orange construction paper (duck and chick)
Pink construction paper (bunny)
1 (1-1/2") white pom-pom (bunny tail)
White acrylic paint
Sponge to apply paint
Miniature flowers, pom-poms, and ribbon
Straw hat for the duck
Glue gun
Easter grass and candies

Draw faces on each roll of tissue. Cut the duck or chick beak and feet from orange construction paper. Cut ears and feet for bunnies from pink construction paper. Glue ears into bunny by spreading the paper enough to snug ears in place. Glue beaks and feet in place. Sponge paint onto feet and ears of bunnies to create the appearance of fur. Push Easter grass and candies in the tube. Decorate with small flowers or pom-poms, a tied ribbon at the neck, and a hat for the duck.

CHOCOLATE EASTER BASKET

Dipping chocolate is easy to use if you take care not to overheat it.

1 pound melted chocolate (dipping chocolate, summer coating, or
   chocolate chips)
Waxed paper
1 large, good-quality balloon
Coconut Grass (optional)
Easter candies (optional)

Cover a large cookie sheet with waxed paper. Blow up the balloon until it's the size and shape you want for your basket. Don't fill the balloon to its full capacity or it may pop when it's dipped in warm chocolate. Tie it closed or use a "bulldog" clip that can hold the balloon closed without tearing it.

Dip the balloon in the chocolate until enough of the balloon is covered to form the basket shape desired. Lift out and allow the excess to drip off, then place the dipped balloon on the waxed paper-covered cookie sheet and cool until hardened.

To remove the balloon from the basket, poke a small pinhole near the top or hold the twisted end closed and remove the clip. Slowly release the air from the balloon. The balloon should pull away from the basket as it deflates. You may have to jiggle the balloon gently away from the bottom.

Decorate the edge of the chocolate basket with Royal Icing using a broad tip on a pastry bag. Bend a large pipe cleaner into a handle shape, place into the frosting, and allow to dry. Fill the basket with Coconut Grass and Easter candy.

ROYAL ICING

3 egg whites, at room temperature
1/2 teaspoon cream of tartar
1 pound confectioners' sugar
Flavoring and food color
   (a little goes a long way)

Beat all the ingredients at high speed for 8 to 10 minutes. This is a hard-drying icing, and must be kept tightly covered at all times. Cover the bowl with a damp cloth or plastic wrap while you are working with it.

How to Melt Chocolate

Cut up the chocolate or coating with a knife or food processor and melt in the top of a double boiler. Fill the bottom of the double boiler with hot water, leaving a 1″ space below the top pan. Stir occasionally.

Chocolate should never be heated to more than 120°F, which is much less than the hand can stand. Never allow water to get into chocolate. Just a little water in chocolate will thicken it so that it cannot be used.

For dipping, it must feel cold to the lips, not just neutral. A chocolate temperature of 88°F is about right, and the room should be 66°F to be ideal. If the temperature is too high, the chocolate will turn grey.

When chocolate is handled right, it may be melted more than once.

EASTER BASKET WITH REAL GRASS

Start this Easter basket at least a week before Easter. It will last for several weeks if you "mow" it regularly with scissors.

Basket
Heavy clear plastic, 6" larger than the inside of the basket
Indoor potting soil
Wheat seed

Line the inside of your basket with plastic and leave at least 6" of excess all the way around. Fill the basket to within an inch of the top with potting soil and pat the soil down firmly. Sprinkle the surface generously with seed, and cover lightly (1/4" to 1/2") with potting soil. Water well, making sure all the seeds are moistened. Pull the excess plastic over the top of the soil to preserve moisture. Set the basket in a warm, sunny spot. In two to three days, the seed will start to sprout, and within a week to ten days, you will have grass.

Decorate the basket with a bow and colored eggs. Add a Spoon Bunny or Easter Veggies. The grass will grow rapidly. Trim with scissors. Use the trimmed grass in sandwiches or salads.

SPOON BUNNIES

Tuck these delightful bunnies into your children's Easter baskets.

6 pastel plastic spoons
Red and black puff paints or permanent markers
1 yard heavy black thread
Glue
6 small pink pom-poms
1 (8-1/2" x 11") rectangle white felt
1 (8-1/2" x 11") rectangle pastel felt (same color as spoons)
6 round suckers
3 yards pastel ribbon
6 (1") white pom-poms or cotton balls

Paint eyes, mouth, and cheeks on the back of each spoon. Let dry. Tie three 1-1/2" strands of heavy black thread together in the middle and glue above the mouth for whiskers. Glue pink pom-pom nose above the whiskers. Cut ears out of the pastel felt, and cut smaller inside ears out of white felt. Glue small white ears on larger pastel ears, and glue to back of head. Place a sucker in the spoon and tie ribbon around the neck. Glue a small white pom-pom or cotton-ball tail on the sucker stick.

Coconut Grass

Place shredded coconut in a jar with a tight-fitting lid. Add 2 to 3 drops of green food coloring and shake vigorously until the coconut is colored. If the color is too bright, add more coconut and shake again. If it's too light, add more food coloring and shake again. Spread the coconut out on waxed paper or plastic wrap to dry before using.

EASTER EGG ANIMALS

Captivate your family with these delightful eggs!

Posterboard (white, pink, and yellow)
1 sheet red construction paper
Scissors
Colored hard-cooked eggs or hollow eggs (see I Love You Eggs)
Glue
Black fine-tip permanent marker
Pink pom-poms or cotton balls (tail)

Enlarge the patterns to make 2″ to 2-1/2″ feet. Use white posterboard for the bunny feet and yellow for the chick feet. Cut bunny ears from white posterboard, inner ears from pink, the chick's beak from yellow, and the chick's crest from red construction paper. Glue the feet, ears, crest, and beak to the egg. Draw facial features with a fine-tip marker. Add a pom-pom or cotton-ball tail to the bunny.

EASTER NECKLACE

This edible necklace is fun for preschoolers to make.

Clear plastic wrap
Easter candies, small toys, tiny Easter baskets
Pastel ribbon

Cut a piece of plastic wrap the length you want your necklace to be, plus 4″. Place items 1″ from the far edge of the wrap at 2″ intervals, leaving 2″ free at each end. Fold the 1″ edge of plastic over the items and then roll toward you until items are entirely wrapped. Tie off the ends and between each item with pastel ribbon. Tie pieces of ribbon to each end to complete the necklace.

EASTER VEGGIES

These colorful craft vegetables can be hidden for your Easter egg hunt, put in Easter baskets, or used in a centerpiece.

Cellophane (clear, red, orange, and purple)
Easter candies and candy corn
Creative twist, green metallic
Raffia or excelsior packing material
Clear tape or florist wire
Glue
Orange felt
Easter grass

ONION

Cut a 5″ x 5″ square of clear cellophane and place light-colored candies in the middle. Bring up all the sides and insert three 6″ lengths of green twist. Secure with tape or wire and cut off overlapping cellophane. For roots, use excelsior or raffia cut in narrow strips and glued in place.

RADISH

Cut a 3″ x 3″ piece of red cellophane and place red jelly beans or red-hot candies in the middle. Bring up all sides and insert three or four 4″ lengths of green twist. Secure with tape or wire. Glue on tiny pieces of excelsior or raffia for roots.

BEET

Follow the directions for the radish, but use various sizes of purple cellophane. Don't fill the cellophane entirely full, but tape around the bottom and clip the leftover cellophane to resemble roots.

CARROT

Cut a 10″ x 10″ x 15″ triangle of orange cellophane and mark the center of the longest side. Roll it into a cone, so that the point of the cone is at that center mark. Place candy corn in the cone and insert three or four 4″ lengths of green twist. Secure with tape or wire.

You can also make a carrot from felt by cutting two identical carrot shapes from orange felt. Glue the edges together and fill with candy. For a curly carrot top, stuff with Easter grass.

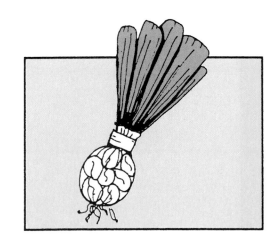

I LOVE YOU EGGS (HOLLOW EGGS)

Personalize your eggs by enclosing special messages in the shells.

Use a sharp needle to poke a small hole in the small end of an egg and a larger hole in the larger end. Through the large hole, puncture the egg yolk with the needle. Hold the egg over a bowl and gently blow through the small hole to force the raw egg out of the shell. Rinse the shells thoroughly.

A turkey baster can also be used to suck the contents from the eggs. Poke only one hole—large enough to accommodate the point of the baster. Be sure to clean the baster with hot soapy water or run it through your dishwasher.

It's best to discard the contents of the eggs. If you insist on using them, cook them as soon as possible, and use only in thoroughly cooked products, such as cakes or custards, not in soft scrambled eggs.

To decorate eggshells, use marking pens, ribbon, lace, and acrylic or watercolor paints. "I Love You" messages can be written on small slips of paper, rolled up, and carefully placed inside the eggs through the larger hole.

EASTER RAIN SUPERSTITION

If it rains on Easter Sunday, it will rain the following seven Sundays!

BREAD CLAY EGG CRITTERS

Wooden eggs are best for this project because they won't break and they won't spoil.

8 slices day-old bread
1/2 cup white craft glue
Wooden, hollow, or hard-cooked eggs
Acrylic paints
Small brush
Glue
Clear varnish spray

Cut the crusts off of the bread slices. In a large bowl, break the bread into small pieces. Add glue a little at a time, kneading with your hands until a smooth, clay-like mixture is formed. This kneading process will take 15 to 20 minutes. When it is smooth and pliable, cover with a damp cloth and set aside.

Apply hand lotion to keep the clay from sticking to your hands. Shape these cute characters, or use your imagination to create some originals. Allow to dry overnight, then paint with a small brush. When completely dry, spray with a clear varnish to seal.

TURTLE

Pinch off a piece of bread clay and flatten into a turtle shell that is about 3″ x 5″ and 3/4″ thick. Press and glue an egg into the center of the clay. Shape feet and head on the turtle. Make holes for eyes with a toothpick.

DUCK

Shape duck feet from bread clay. Glue an egg on top of the feet to form the duck's body. Shape small pieces of clay into wings, head, and bill, and glue them to the egg.

BEAR

Shape bread clay into bear feet. Glue an egg on top. Shape ears, head, and paws from clay and glue in place.

DINOSAUR

Shape a head, back, and tail from bread clay to resemble the dinosaur of your choice and glue onto an egg.

EASTER EGG TREE

Decorate this tree with flowers and Hatching Chick and Bunny Ornaments.

A tree limb with many smaller branches
Spray paint (optional)
Plaster of Paris
Basket with plastic liner (large enough to hold the branch)
Easter grass
Tiny silk flowers
Glue gun

Spray paint the branch if desired. Mix the plaster in the plastic liner according to package directions. Insert the tree branch in the plaster and allow to harden. Put the plastic liner inside the basket and cover the plaster with grass. Attach the flowers to the branch with glue gun. Hang Hatching Chick and Bunny Ornaments on the tree.

Pace Egging

In English villages, children carried on an old sport called pace-egging. The name comes from *Pasch*, the word that means Easter in most European countries. This derives from *Pesach*, the Hebrew Passover, which falls at the same time of the year.

Pace-eggers were much like Halloween trick-or-treaters. They went from house to house in costumes or with paper streamers and bright ribbons attached to their clothes. With faces blackened or masked, they sang or performed skits and demanded pace-eggs, either colored hard-cooked eggs or substitutes such as candy and small coins.

WHITE EASTER SUPERSTITION

A white Christmas brings a green Easter, and a green Christmas brings a white Easter!

HATCHING CHICK AND BUNNY ORNAMENTS

Store these cute chicks and funny bunnies in an open egg carton inside a Styrofoam-popcorn-filled box.

CHICKS

6 raw eggs
12 (2") yellow pom-poms (for heads and bodies)
12 (1/8"–1/4") wiggly craft eyes
Orange felt, cut in six 3/8" triangles (for beaks)
1 yard narrow pink ribbon, cut into six 5" strips
Glue gun

BUNNIES

6 raw eggs
12 (2") pink pom-poms (for heads and bodies)
12 (1/8"–1/4") wiggly craft eyes
Pink felt, cut in bunny ear shapes
White felt, cut smaller for inside bunny ears
1 yard narrow pink ribbon, cut into six 5" strips
12 (1/4") light pink pom-poms
6 (1/8") white pom-poms
Glue gun

To make each ornament, cup an egg in your hand and tap firmly with a knife to crack the shell. Break the egg in half. Wash both halves of the shell and allow to dry thoroughly. Glue the ends of the ribbon inside the larger half of the eggshell on opposite sides to form a handle. Glue the head and body pom-poms together, and attach the eyes. Glue felt beaks on the chicks.

For the bunnies, glue two small pink pom-poms side by side on the head for cheeks and glue the small white pom-pom in the middle of the cheeks.

Glue the smaller white felt ears to the larger pink felt ears. Glue the ears to the top of the head.

Set a completed chick or bunny inside the larger half of the eggshell. Glue the smaller end of the egg to the chick's head to make it appear as if it were just hatching.

T I P : If you don't have any wiggly eyes, punch out black construction paper with a round hole punch and glue to slightly larger round pieces of white construction paper.

SPRING BUNNY HATS

This makes a great door decoration or wall hanging.

1 large hat
1/2 of a hat, one size smaller than the large hat
Paint (recommended: American Acrylic Paints)
    White (White Wash)
    Blue (Country Blue)
    Dark Pink (Boysenberry)
    Light Pink (Baby Pink)
    Black (Ebony Black)
2 (1") wiggly eyes (optional)
1 (2") pink pom-pom (optional)
1" sponge brush
#8 flat brush
Small sponge
Liner brush
1 (8-1/2" x 11") rectangle pink felt or fun foam
Raffia
Wire
Spanish moss
Spring flowers or vegetables
2 yards (2" wide) ribbon
Wire for hanging
Glue

Paint the rounded part of the larger hat (excluding the brim) white. With the #8 flat brush, paint a dark pink triangle on the center of the hat. Sponge cheeks on sides of nose with dark pink. Highlight cheeks and nose with light pink. Draw blue eyes. Paint the lines around the eyes, nose, mouth, whiskers, and the centers of the eyes with black. Let dry. Highlight eyes with white. (If your hand is not steady, or you prefer not to paint eyes and nose, hot glue pink pom-pom nose in the center of the hat and wiggly eyes above the nose.)

Cut rabbit ears out of felt or fun foam, 11" long, 3" wide, and tapered at the ends. Glue the ears to the sides of the head so that the glue will be hidden under the hat when the hat is glued on. Glue the small half hat onto the head.

To make hair, wrap raffia around a 4" piece of cardboard, slide it off, and wrap wire around the middle. Glue raffia hair under the brim of the smaller hat. Glue Spanish moss across the top brim of the smaller hat. Glue spring flowers or vegetables into moss. Tie the ribbon into a bow and glue under the chin of the bunny. Glue a wire to the back to hang.

Easter Egg Tips

- A fresh egg's shelf life in the refrigerator is about four to five weeks beyond the date it was packed.

- As the egg ages, moisture evaporates and the egg sac becomes smaller, leaving more air inside the shell. That's why eggs that are "not too fresh" are easier to peel.

- Always refrigerate an egg with the large end up. The yolk will center when hard-cooked and make a better presentation when sliced or halved for deviled eggs.

- To make sure all the eggs cook evenly, cook them in a single layer in a wide pan or in batches.

- To hard-cook eggs, place the eggs in a saucepan and cover with cold water. Bring to a boil and remove from the heat. Cover and let stand. It takes about 15 minutes to hard cook Large eggs by this method. Let Medium eggs stand about 3 minutes less. Let Extra Large eggs stand about 3 minutes more, and let Jumbo eggs stand about 6 minutes more.

- Never boil eggs. They'll be tough and rubbery with a greenish ring around the yolk.

- A little food coloring in the water will help distinguish hard-cooked eggs from fresh eggs.

- Plunge hard-cooked eggs into cold water while they're hot. This will stop the cooking process and prevent a greenish ring from forming around the egg yolks, and it will make the eggs easier to peel.

- Refrigerate and use uncracked hard-cooked eggs within a week. Leave them in their shells—the shells are nature's own protective packaging.

- For easy peeling, crack the shell all over by tapping it gently on the table or countertop. Then roll it back and forth between your hands to loosen the cracked shell. Since the egg's air cell is usually in the large end of the egg, start to peel there. It may help to hold the egg under cold running water or dip it in a bowl of water.

EASTER EGG HUNT

Easter eggs are symbolic of the rebirth of new life in spring and Christ's resurrection.

Assign each child a color. Buy plastic eggs or color hard-cooked eggs in an equal number of each color. Fill plastic eggs with candy or small toys. Hide the eggs according to the age and ability of the child. If you have several children coming to the egg hunt, a time-saving tip and a fun idea is to have the older children hide eggs for the younger children. Eggs for very young children can be *hidden* so that they can be seen, but eggs for older children can be hidden in more challenging locations. Give each child an empty basket with a ribbon of the appropriate color tied to the handle.

Make it an extra fun Easter Treasure Hunt by including messages. You can put a clue inside a plastic egg, write it on the outside of the egg with a fine-tipped marker, or hollow the egg shell and insert a rolled message. Place the egg containing the first message in the child's Easter basket.

EASTER EGG GAMES

Egg rolling, a custom several hundred years old, is a favorite game that recalls the stone being rolled away from Christ's tomb.

- Roll hard-cooked eggs on a field, crashing them into each other, until only one unbroken egg remains.
- Roll hard-cooked or raw eggs down a hill. The winner is the one whose egg doesn't crack.
- Divide into teams of two people, with one egg per team. Toss eggs, standing a foot further apart with each toss, until the egg breaks. The last unbroken egg wins.

HAIRY EGGHEADS

Don't let your eggs go around bald.

Gently crack off the top quarter of a raw egg. Empty and rinse the eggshell well. Draw a face on the hollow shell with marking pens or paint. Fill the shell with damp potting soil. Sprinkle alfalfa seeds on top and gently press them into the dirt. Keep the soil moist, but not wet. Set the egg on a sunny windowsill. Within 5 to 8 days, your egg will grow a lush "head of hair."

Keep Easter Eggs Safe

- Because the eggshell is still porous, keep hands and surfaces that touch hard-cooked eggs clean. Harmful bacteria can get inside through the shell and multiply to dangerous levels if conditions are ideal.

- To keep colored eggs safe for your Easter Egg Hunt, put each egg in a small plastic sandwich bag or wrap in plastic wrap and tie it shut.

- Keep eggs chilled (before and after dying them) until you are ready to hide them. If they're not found within about five hours, discard them.

- If you aren't going to eat the eggs within the five-hour safe period, refrigerate them up to a total of four or five days.

PIONEER EASTER EGGS

Have fun dying eggs the way the pioneers did!

Raw eggs
Onionskins
Greens such as carrot tops, celery leaves, parsley, spinach, or dandelion
  greens
Thread

Your supermarket produce manager will probably give you a bag full of loose onionskins. Place several handfuls in water and bring to a boil. Reduce heat and simmer for 5 minutes. Put in the refrigerator to cool. Wrap the raw eggs in the greens and bind them tightly with thread. Designs will be printed only where the greens are firmly pressed against the eggs.

Gently lower the eggs into the cooled onionskin water and bring the water back to a boil. Remove from heat, cover, and let stand 15 minutes. (See Easter Egg Tips.)

Plunge eggs into cold water until cool enough to handle. Remove threads and leaves. You'll be delighted to see the interesting designs!

LATIN PROVERB
Omne vivum ex ovo—
"All life comes from an egg."

DEVILED EGGS

Finely chopped almonds give these deviled eggs a nice crunch.

6 hard-cooked eggs
1/4 cup mayonnaise
1 teaspoon Dijon mustard
1 tablespoon very finely chopped white or green onions
2 tablespoons finely chopped slivered almonds
2 tablespoons finely grated Cheddar cheese
Salt and pepper to taste
Dash paprika
12 whole roasted almonds

Cut the eggs in half lengthwise and remove the yolks. Place the yolks, mayonnaise, mustard, onions, chopped almonds, cheese, salt, and pepper in a quart-sized plastic bag. Close the bag and knead until the contents are thoroughly blended. Push the contents toward one corner. Snip about 1/4" off the corner of the bag. Squeeze the bag gently and fill the egg whites with the yolk mixture. (Or, combine the ingredients in a bowl and spoon the mixture into the egg whites.) Sprinkle with paprika and garnish with whole almonds. Cover and refrigerate until ready to serve. Makes 12 egg halves.

President James Madison started the "White House Egg Roll" during his presidency in 1809. The annual event draws thousands of people to the White House lawn where children roll eggs down a slight slope south of the Truman balcony.

EGG SAILBOATS

Children love to eat these tiny boats.

6 hard-cooked eggs, peeled
6 slices of American cheese
12 toothpicks

Cut the eggs in half lengthwise. Cut the cheese slices in half diagonally to form triangular sails and skewer each on a toothpick mast. Stick the toothpick into the egg to form a boat.

EGG POSY

Grown-ups like this flower as much as children do!

1 hard-cooked egg, peeled
Salad dressing
1 cherry tomato
1 slice of American cheese
1 slice of toast
Celery leaves

Cut the egg into thin, round slices. Arrange the egg slices in a circular flower pattern with the egg-slice petals overlapping slightly. Spoon your favorite salad dressing in the middle of the circle, and top with a cherry tomato half for the center of the flower. Cut the slice of cheese to form leaves. Add a thin slice of toast for a stem. Arrange celery leaves around the base of the stem.

EGG DIP

Here's a great way to use some of your Easter eggs.

6 hard-cooked eggs, finely chopped
1/3 cup reduced fat mayonnaise
1 tablespoon lemon juice
1 teaspoon prepared mustard
1 teaspoon Worcestershire sauce
Salt and pepper to taste

Mix all the ingredients together and serve as a dip for fresh vegetables. Makes 1-3/4 cups.

EASTER BUNNY CAKE

This cake is almost too cute to eat!

1 (8"–9") round cake, baked
4 cups white frosting
1 pink SnoBall snack cake
Posterboard (ears)
Black and pink candies (eyes and nose)
Black licorice strips (mouth and whiskers)
2 cups coconut

Cut the cake in half. Turn one half over and frost the bottom, flat side. Put the other half on top of the frosting, so that the two halves form a sandwich with the flat sides together. Stand the cake up, with the cut edge on the plate. Glue the cake to the plate with some frosting. Frost the cake.

Make the ears from posterboard. Cut a slit in the cake and insert the ears. Use the SnoBall for the tail and the licorice strips for mouth and whiskers. Use pink and black candies for the nose and eyes. For coconut lovers, sprinkle coconut all over cake to make a furry bunny.

Earth Day

APRIL 22

The first Earth Day was held in 1970. This holiday is intended to create an awareness of the limited resources of our earth and to remind people that they are responsible for the condition of the earth and its future.

The theme of the first Earth Day in 1970 was "Give Earth a Chance." We each need to do our part to keep our earth clean and beautiful.

- Write to the Environmental Protection Agency for information on what you and your family can do for the environment. There may be an office near you, or you can write:

    United States Environmental Protection Agency
    Office of Public Affairs
    401 M Street, SW
    Washington, DC 20460

- Organize a family or neighborhood clean-up for a local park, beach, or other public area.

- Start a recycling program at school or work.

- Buy goods in recyclable containers.

- Recycle things at home by creating new uses for them.
    - Decorate a tuna can to hold paper clips or rubber bands.
    - Use the bottom half of a gallon plastic milk jug for a leak-proof potted plant holder.
    - Make wind chimes out of enamel painted metal lids.

- Compost all of your kitchen scraps. Your garden will grow better, you'll save on your garbage bill, and you'll decrease the waste in your local landfill.

Arbor Day

The Latin word for tree is *arbor*, and Arbor Day was first celebrated on April 10, 1872, in Nebraska with the planting of over one million trees. Dates vary depending on the planting season, but this holiday is celebrated the world over to call awareness to the conservation of our natural resources.

Give Mother Nature a helping hand and plant a tree or build a birdhouse in honor of the bountiful gifts of nature.

PLANT A TREE!

Hold a family tree-planting ceremony. Go to a nursery or tree farm and have each family member select a sapling for your yard. Take pictures planting the trees and of each family member with his or her tree. Chart the trees as they grow, recording rainy days, watering, and fertilizing your trees. Take pictures each year with family members next to their trees.

COCONUT BIRD FEEDER

When the fresh coconut is gone, keep this little bird feeder filled with seed.

1 coconut
Heavy-gauge wire

Poke small holes in the top of the coconut and drain out the milk. Cut a hole approximately 2″ in diameter on the side of the coconut. Pull the wire through the holes in the top of the coconut and hang from a tree. Birds will fly inside and eat the coconut.

BIRD TRAIL MIX

A "trail mix" just for your feathered friends.

Shallow plastic margarine container with lid
Heavy-gauge wire
3 empty thread spools
Sunflower seeds
Birdseed
Raisins
Cracked corn

Poke small holes for drainage in the bottom of the container. Make a hole in the center, large enough to accommodate the wire. Bend the end of the wire so it won't pull through the hole. Thread the empty spools onto the wire. Poke a hole in the center of the plastic lid and thread onto wire. Make a loop on the end of the wire to fit over a tree branch. Fill container with seeds, raisins, and corn and hang.

PINECONE SUET

This tasty treat will draw birds from all over the neighborhood.

1/2 cup bacon grease
1 tablespoon peanut butter
1/2 cup cornmeal
1 pinecone
1/4 cup birdseed
Wire or string

Attach wire or string firmly to pinecone. Mix bacon grease, peanut butter, and cornmeal together. Push the mixture up into and all over the pinecone. Roll the pinecone in birdseed and hang.

MAY

May is a month for remembering special people: our mothers and those who died in defense of our country. Although both of these holidays are relatively new American holidays, they both have ancient origins. Almost every culture has had observances to honor their deceased, and a day to honor mothers traces back to ancient Greece.

Mothers young and old appreciate handmade gifts, and this chapter contains ideas for gifts that any mother would love to receive. Plan ahead to give mom the day off. Let her sleep late, then serve breakfast in bed with a personalized card on the tray. Make her a special gift for the garden or one that brings flowers indoors. And don't forget that Mother's Day lasts *all day*. Do all the chores, including getting stuff ready for school the next day. Let Mom sit back and realize what a wonderful family she has.

On Memorial Day, remember veterans and loved ones by attending a parade, going to the local veterans' home, or visiting graves. Make a Family Memory Book to record special things about your ancestors and extended family.

Memorial Day also marks the beginning of summer. Kick it off right with great recipes and decorations featuring some of the fresh watermelons that start appearing in the markets during May.

Mother's Day

Mothers have been honored on special days since early Greek and Roman times. The founder of Mother's Day in the United States is Miss Anna Jarvis of Philadelphia. Although never a mother herself, Miss Jarvis spent her life trying to make sure that one day a year would be set aside to honor mothers. She also started the custom of wearing a flower on Mother's Day.

Mother's Day became an official American holiday in 1914 when a resolution was introduced into Congress which recognized that ". . . the service rendered by the American mothers is the greatest source of the country's strength and inspiration. . . ."

President Wilson officially proclaimed the day as a ". . . public expression of our love and reverence for the mothers of our country . . ." and ordered the national flag to be displayed.

Carnations have become symbolic of Mother's Day, because in the "language of flowers" carnations stand for sweetness, purity, and endurance—qualities often associated with mothers. Red carnations are worn to honor living mothers, and white ones to honor the dead.

Mother's Day is one of the most widely celebrated holidays of the year, perhaps because mothers are so special. Show your mother just how much she means to you.

HANDPRINT STEPPING-STONES

Make this an annual Mother's Day event to record your child's growth.

Large plastic bucket
1 (40 pound) bag of premixed concrete (requiring only water)
Water
Shovel or large stick (to mix cement)
1 (16-3/4" x 12" x 3 1/2") foil pan
Board (for leveling cement)
Petroleum jelly

Mix enough cement and water in the bucket to fill the foil pan, following proportions listed on the bag. Pour the cement into the pan. Level the cement and smooth the surface with the side of the board.

Cover the child's hands with petroleum jelly and press them into the cement, then sign and date it. You may also want to have your child draw a picture in the cement with a stick.

When the cement sets, turn the pan over and the block will pop out. Use the cement blocks as stepping-stones in the backyard or as garden art to preserve your child's handiwork. You'll be amazed how often children will place their hands over the imprints to measure their growth.

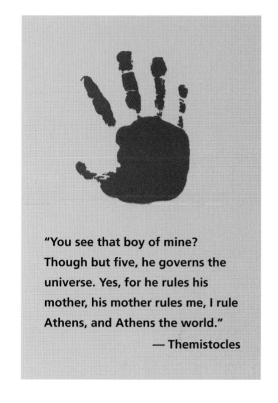

"You see that boy of mine? Though but five, he governs the universe. Yes, for he rules his mother, his mother rules me, I rule Athens, and Athens the world."
— Themistocles

MOTHER'S DAY POP-UP CARD

Use your imagination to make a personalized Mother's Day card. Sometimes the strangest shapes make the cutest cards.

2 (8-1/2" x 11") pieces of cardstock
Pencil
Scissors
Rubber cement
Crayons, markers, colored paper, paper doilies, cotton balls, etc.

Fold each piece of paper in half. Set one aside to be used later as the outside of the card.

Place the paper so that the folded edge is on your left. Mark a large triangle on the bottom left corner. Draw and cut a curved line from the folded edge to the triangle line. Fold along the triangle line between the cut and the point of the triangle. Fold the other direction along the same crease.

Open the card and pull the cut middle pop-up piece toward you. Firmly crease the fold lines so that the pop-up piece points toward you.

Glue the inside and outside of the card together. Be careful not to apply glue on the pop-up area of card.

Turn your creativity loose to decorate the card. You can follow one of these suggestions or design your own.

FLOWER CARD

Turn the card upside down, so that the pop-up forms a vase. Draw, color, and cut flowers out of colored paper and glue them into the vase. Decorate the front of the card with flowers. Write "Mother, every time I see a beautiful flower, I think of you" inside.

ANGEL CARD

Make the triangle pop up into the robe of an angel. Use paper doilies for the wings. Glue paper feet onto the bottom of the triangle and write "You are my Guardian Angel." On the front of your card write "Mother" and draw some clouds or glue some pieces of cotton balls to look like clouds.

NOSE CARD

On the inside of the card, draw a self-portrait using the pop-up triangle as your nose and write "Everybody nose, but I just had to tell you again." Write "Mother, I Love You!" on the front.

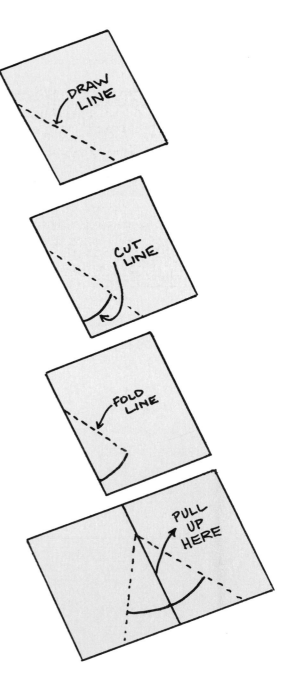

FLOWERS IN LINEN AND LACE

If you can't find a decorative handkerchief that you like, embroider your own.

*Linen napkin or handkerchief (12" x 12") with one
    decorative or embroidered corner*
Heavyweight nonwoven interfacing (12" x 12")
Ruler
Scissors
Glue gun and glue sticks or needle and thread
Quilter's or disappearing fabric marker
11" length (1/4"–1/2" wide) ribbon
Decorative ribbon and dried or silk flowers
Buttons, beads, etc. (optional)

Cut a piece of interfacing the same size as the napkin
or handkerchief. Mark the centers of two adjacent
sides of the interfacing. Fold between these two
marks and stitch 1/4" from the folded edge. The
decorative corner of the napkin or handkerchief,
along with the folded edge of the interfacing, will
become the top of the flower holder.

Place the interfacing on the wrong side of the napkin. Put the folded corner of the interfacing up, and
leave the decorative corner of the napkin exposed.
Stitch a 1/4" seam along the sides, leaving only the
folded corner open. Turn and press.

Fold the bottom corner up toward the interfacing 3" and press.
Divide the bottom folded edge into thirds (approximately 1-1/2"
each) and mark. Mark the top of the napkin 1" above the folded edge
of the interfacing on each side.

Fold each side between the mark along the bottom and the mark
above the interfacing. Crease the folds so that the result is a cone-
shaped holder. Pin in place. Check to see that the cone is symmetrical
and there is no opening in the bottom of the holder. Glue (or hand
stitch) the bottom and outside edges in place.

When the glue is cool, turn the cone over and fold the decorative
corner of the handkerchief down toward the center and press. Stitch
or glue ribbon to the outside top edges of the cone to hang. Glue
on decorative ribbon, buttons, beads, etc. Fill the cone with silk or
dried flowers.

"'Where's Mother?' could be
heard through the hallway. And
they stood and watched her as
she went on alone, and the gates
closed after her. And they said:
'We cannot see her, but she is
with us still. A mother like ours is
more than a memory. She is a
Living Presence.'"

— Temple Bailey

MOM'S GARDEN GLOVE

1 garden glove
Heavy cardboard (3" x 5")
Acrylic paints or permanent markers
Cotton batting
Heavy black wire (24" length), also called
*   "baling wire"*
1 (1/4") dowel or pencil
Packets of vegetable seeds
Small stuffed animals
Small clay pot
Silk flowers
Silk greens
Spanish moss
Dried flowers
1 yard (1"–2" wide) ribbon
Raffia
Glue gun
Wire cutters

Lightly sketch "I Love My Garden" or "Welcome To My Garden!" on the front of the glove in pencil. Paint with acrylics or markers.

Allowing the cardboard to extend 1" above the glove, glue one side of the cardboard to the back inside of the glove. The cardboard will help hold all the things you glue inside the glove. Lightly stuff the fingers and palm with cotton batting.

Twist the wire around the dowel or pencil, forming random loops. Slide the wire off the dowel. Bend the wire into an arch and hot glue to each side of the inside of the glove.

Arrange other items attractively and hot glue in place. The seed packets will be glued to the cardboard so they show, high enough to cover the cardboard. Fill in any bare spots with Spanish moss. Tie raffia or ribbon around the wristband.

The home where happiness
    securely dwells
Was never wrought by charms
    or magic spells.
A mother made it beautiful,
    but knew
No magic save what toiling
    hands can do.
    —Arthur Wallace Peach

DIRT DESSERT

If you want to have fun with your children, serve them Dirt Dessert!

1 large (5.1 ounce) package instant vanilla pudding mix
3 cups cold milk
1 large (8 ounce) container frozen whipped topping, thawed
1 (6 ounce) package miniature chocolate chips
1 new child's sand bucket and shovel, cleaned thoroughly,
    or plastic cups or new flowerpot
1 large package Oreo cookies, crushed to crumb consistency
Gummi worms

Mix the pudding according to package directions and allow to set for a few minutes. Fold in the whipped topping and chocolate chips. Put half of the pudding mixture in the bucket. Top with half of the cookie crumbs. Layer with the rest of the pudding and top with cookie crumbs. Add Gummi worms and chill. Use the shovel to serve.

Decorate the bucket with fabric flowers and ribbon. Add a Happy Mother's Day note. Serves 6.

Memorial Day

Memorial Day was first officially celebrated on May 30, 1868, and was called "Decoration Day." The Grand Army organized the celebration at Arlington National Cemetery, and several other communities across the country joined in. In an attempt to heal the bitterness between the North and South, its purpose was to honor the dead of both the Confederate and Union armies who had died in the Civil War.

Decoration Day was changed to Memorial Day in 1971 by President Nixon and became a national holiday. It is a day to remember the soldiers who have died defending our country and ". . . a day of prayer for permanent peace. . . ." Flags fly at half-mast and families remember loved ones who were killed in the two World Wars, Korea, and Vietnam. Services are held at sea for those who died while fighting on the waterways. In Arlington Cemetery, Virginia, there are special services at the Tomb of the Unknown Soldier.

There are usually military and civic parades, and families take flowers to the graves of loved ones. Memorial Day has evolved into a holiday to remember not only those who died in wars, but all of the ancestors and family members we have lost.

Some of the best-known songs have been inspired by wars. Learning these songs is a great way to explore history because it gives you a better idea of what people felt during these events. Check out your library for collections of these songs and practice them with your family and friends. Then you might want to visit a retirement home. The residents will enjoy your concert and might even teach *you* some terrific new songs!

Along with the solemn activities of Memorial Day, have fun with the family because the children are out of school for the day! Remember that it also marks the beginning of the summer season—fresh fruit, home-made ice cream, and vacations.

FAMILY MEMORY BOOK

This is a good opportunity to learn more about your family.

Memorial Day is the perfect time to start a Family Memory Book. Make a page for each family member who has died. Use a loose-leaf binder so that you can add pages each year.

If you're one of the lucky people whose immediate family is still living, your parents or grandparents will remember their own parents, brothers, sisters, aunts, uncles and grandparents. It will also mean a lot to the older members of your family to know that the people they were close to are not forgotten.

Write down the facts at the top of the page, including their name, where and when they were born and died, and how they were related to you. If they had a spouse or children, also include their names. Then write things you or another member of the family can remember about that person and what made them special.

Your book won't ever be finished. Memorial Day is a good time to look at your Family Memory Book and add pages to it. You can also make copies of the pages for other family members. They will be delighted that you want to share your memories of the people they loved.

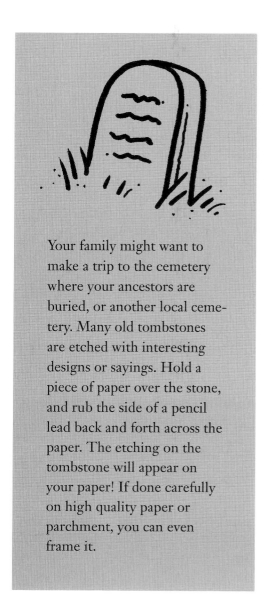

Your family might want to make a trip to the cemetery where your ancestors are buried, or another local cemetery. Many old tombstones are etched with interesting designs or sayings. Hold a piece of paper over the stone, and rub the side of a pencil lead back and forth across the paper. The etching on the tombstone will appear on your paper! If done carefully on high quality paper or parchment, you can even frame it.

WATERMELON SLUSH

If you like watermelon, you'll love this refreshing concoction!

3 cups water
2 cups sugar
1 (12 ounce) can frozen orange juice concentrate
1 (6 ounce) can frozen lemonade concentrate
1 (6 ounce) can pineapple juice concentrate
3 ripe bananas, mashed
1 (1/4 ounce) package unsweetened strawberry Kool-Aid
1/2 gallon watermelon juice

Mix the water and sugar in a saucepan and boil until sugar is dissolved. In a large bowl, mix orange, lemonade, and pineapple concentrates and mashed bananas. Add sugar water to the concentrate mixture and stir until frozen concentrates are blended. Pour into freezer containers. Remove from freezer about 1 hour before serving to soften. Add Kool-Aid and watermelon juice. Serve in a watermelon carved like a punch bowl. Makes 14 cups.

(Note: To make watermelon juice, de-seed 1 large watermelon and push meat through a strainer or juice extractor.)

WHALE OF A DESSERT

You can use any variety of melon to make this table decoration.

Watermelon
Posterboard
Dish towel
Oblong glass dish, large enough for melon
Magic marker
Sparkler (where legal) or long paper candles
Dry ice

Draw a whale face on one end of the melon. Cut the tail from a piece of posterboard, using the pattern. Make a slit at the back end of the melon and insert the edge of the tail. Roll up the dish towel lengthwise and form it into a circle. Place the towel in the dish to keep the melon from rolling. Set the melon on the towel. Insert a lighted sparkler or candle in the top of the melon for the spout. Place small pieces of dry ice around the melon and pour warm water over the dry ice to create a fog. The mist will float around the whale!

How to De-Seed a Watermelon

Cut both ends off the watermelon and set it on its end inside a large dish to catch the juice. Place the point of a paring knife just into the seeds and cut the melon from top to bottom, about 3″ deep. Repeat all the way around the watermelon, creating wedges about 3″–4″ apart.

With the palm of your hand, hit the melon up and down along each wedge until the wedge is loose. The seed base is the weakest point of the watermelon, and with a little encouragement, the rind and meat will naturally separate there. Remove the wedge and scrape out the watermelon seeds.

Whale tail pattern

SHERBET WATERMELON

You can even eat the "seeds"!

Lime sherbet
Raspberry sherbet
Chocolate chips

Line a round glass bowl with plastic wrap. Spoon softened lime sherbet around the bottom and sides, 3/4" thick, smoothing as you go. Let harden in the freezer. Mix softened raspberry sherbet and chocolate chips together and spoon inside lime sherbet rind. Freeze for 1-1/2 hours. Unmold, remove plastic wrap, and slice like a watermelon.

KICK-THE-CAN ICE CREAM

Make your dessert and play a game of kick-the-can at the same time!

3/4 cup whole milk
1/2 teaspoon vanilla
1 cup cream
1/3 cup sugar
Flavoring (chocolate syrup, raspberries, strawberries, etc.)
1 (1 pound) can and 1 (3 pound) can with lids (one fits inside the other)
3/4 cup salt or rock salt
Crushed ice

Blend the milk, vanilla, cream, sugar, and flavoring and pour in the smaller can; secure the lid. Put the small can inside the big can. Fill the big can with rock salt and ice. Put the lid on the big can. Roll the can with your foot for 5 minutes. Drain off water, then add more salt and ice to the large can and roll 5 to 8 minutes more. Serves 3 to 4.

DOUBLE-DECKER COOKIES

These two recipes are also great as singles!

Prepare dough for Peanut Butter Crunchers and Oatmeal Crisps. Form balls of peanut butter mixture about 1-1/4″ in diameter. Butter your hands with shortening or oil and flatten the cookie dough balls on a cookie sheet with your fingers, leaving shallow ridges. Press a ball of oatmeal dough on top of peanut butter dough. Bake at 350°F until golden brown, about 8 to 10 minutes. Cool on rack. Makes 5 to 6 dozen.

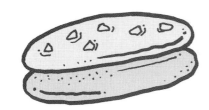

(Note: Follow the same baking directions when making these recipes individually.)

PEANUT BUTTER CRUNCHERS

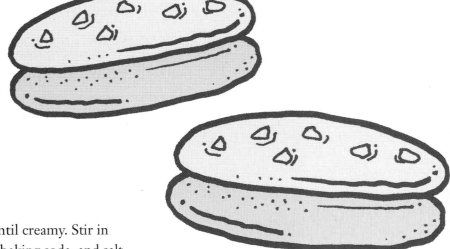

3/4 cup butter or margarine
3/4 cup brown sugar
1/2 cup granulated sugar
1 egg
1 teaspoon vanilla
3/4 cup crunchy peanut butter
1-3/4 cups all-purpose flour
1/2 teaspoon baking soda
1/4 teaspoon salt

Beat butter or margarine and sugars together until creamy. Stir in egg, vanilla, and peanut butter. Combine flour, baking soda, and salt in a separate bowl and add to mixture. Stir until mixed.

OATMEAL CRISPS

1 cup butter or margarine
1 cup brown sugar
1 cup granulated sugar
2 eggs
1 teaspoon vanilla
1-1/2 cups all-purpose flour
1 teaspoon baking soda
1 teaspoon salt
3 cups oatmeal
1 cup chocolate chips

Beat butter or margarine and sugars until creamy. Stir in eggs and vanilla. Combine flour, baking soda and salt in a separate bowl and then add to the mixture. Stir in oatmeal and chocolate chips. Stir until mixed.

JUNE

Although neither of the two major holidays in June are national legal holidays, both are regularly observed throughout the United States. Each year Presidential Proclamations are issued to recognize Flag Day and Father's Day.

Both holidays are also quite recent. Flag Day has only been presidentially proclaimed since 1941, and Father's Day since 1966. The law that requires an annual Presidential Proclamation for Father's Day wasn't enacted until 1972!

Flag Day is a day set aside to honor the *Stars and Stripes*, and can be a fun day to celebrate some of our nation's history. Treat your family to a colorful flag cake, or use the day to find out more about flags and design your own. Since Betsy Ross is so strongly tied to the flag in American folklore, you might want to look ahead to July and make a fun Betsy Ross decoration.

Father's Day is the major holiday in June. Treat your dad to breakfast in bed, followed with any of the handmade gifts in this chapter. Dad will have the office in hysterics when he wears a snake tie filled with candy! You may want to throw an outdoor barbecue in his honor. July and September also have some wonderful recipes and decorations for outdoor cooking, so peek ahead to get some ideas on how to make Father's Day memorable!

Flag Day

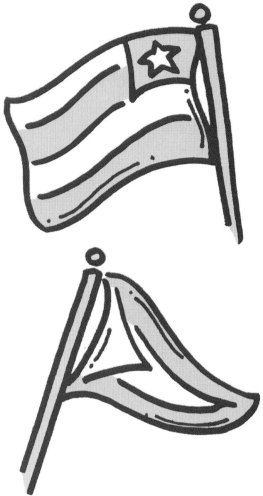

On June 14, 1777, in Philadelphia, the second Continental Congress adopted a design for an American flag. Betsy Ross is credited with sewing the first *Stars and Stripes*, with "thirteen stripes, alternate red and white" and "thirteen stars, white in a blue field, representing a new constellation." George Washington said: "We take the stars from heaven, the red from our mother country, separating it by white stripes, thus showing that we have separated from her, and the white stripes shall go down to posterity, representing liberty."

The original plan was to add a new star and a new stripe every time a state came into the union. In 1918, President James Monroe signed a bill that declared the official United States flag would again have only thirteen stripes and that a new star would be added on the Fourth of July after each new state became part of the union. The most recent additions to the flag were for Alaska in 1959 and Hawaii in 1960.

In 1877, one hundred years after the flag was adopted, Congress declared that the flag should be flown over public buildings on June 14, and in 1916, President Woodrow Wilson proclaimed that Flag Day be observed on June 14. But Flag Day didn't become a national holiday until August 3, 1949, when President Harry S. Truman signed the National Flag Day Bill.

At 7:00 pm EDT, there is a *Pause for the Pledge* as part of the National Flag Day ceremonies. The concept of a pause for the Pledge of Allegiance was conceived as a way for all citizens to simultaneously share a patriotic moment. Share this moment with your family and the nation.

On Flag Day, the red, white, and blue banner is displayed across the nation, from all public buildings and from many homes and businesses. Purchase a flag to fly outside your home. Start an annual family tradition by serving this Old Glory Cake.

OLD GLORY CAKE

A glorious cake to see!

1 (9" x 13") sheet cake
White frosting
1 (21 ounce) can blueberry pie filling
1 (21 ounce) can cherry pie filling or 2 pints fresh strawberries, sliced
Pastry bag and tip

Frost cake with white frosting. Spread blueberry pie filling over a rectangle in the upper left corner. Arrange cherry pie filling or strawberry slices across remainder of cake to form seven stripes. Dot 13 white-icing stars in a circle on the blue background. Fill in borders and white stripes with frosting.

Have some fun designing your own flags. Research what the various colors and symbols mean and try different combinations. You might even make it a big group project and design a flag for your family or school, or just create some flag postcards to send to friends.

Father's Day

America seems to be unique in its honoring of fathers on a special day, and it hasn't been observed as long as most holidays. It's amazing how often more than one person may think of the same idea at about the same time. Mrs. Charles Clayton of Fairmont, West Virginia, requested that her minister, Dr. Robert Webb, conduct a Father's Day service on July 5, 1908. Mrs. Dodd suggested it in Washington in 1909. In 1911, the idea came up in Chicago and in 1912, in Vancouver, Washington.

Louise Smart Dodd of Spokane, Washington, may have been the most influential promoter of Father's Day. Louise's mother had died giving birth to her sixth child, leaving William Smart to raise six young children all by himself. Mrs. Dodd and her minister promoted the idea of a day honoring fathers, and presented a petition to the Spokane Ministerial Association, asking that one Sunday in June (the month of her father's birth) be selected. The ministers agreed, and the YMCA helped sponsor the event. The mayor of Spokane issued the first Father's Day proclamation, and Governor Hay set the third Sunday in June for the statewide observance.

Another important figure in the "honor fathers" movement was Harry Meek. In 1915, as president of the Chicago Uptown Lions Club, he suggested the third Sunday in June (the Sunday nearest his own birthday) as Father's Day. The Lions crowned him "Originator of Father's Day."

In 1916, President Wilson pressed a button at his desk in the White House that unfurled a flag in Spokane and began a celebration. In 1924, President Calvin Coolidge recommended that Father's Day be noted in all the states, declaring that "the widespread observance of this occasion is calculated to establish more intimate relationships between fathers and their children, and also to impress upon fathers the full measure of their obligations."

It wasn't until 1972 that the day was finally established permanently when President Richard Nixon signed a Congressional resolution and put Father's Day on the same continuing basis as Mother's Day.

Father works hard all year, and today is his special day. Give him a gift that will remind him of your love and appreciation all year long! You may also want to make some of these fun gifts for other important *dads* in your life—a grandpa, favorite uncle or godfather.

SNAKE TIE

Fill this snake with tasty "eggs"!

An old necktie
Scissors
Green felt (8-1/2" x 11")
Needle and thread
Cotton balls
Small wiggly craft eyes
Grosgrain ribbon
Red felt
Velcro (3" x 1")
"Eggs" (M&M's, jelly beans, or small candies)

Cut the large end off an old necktie, forming a squared end.

Draw a pattern in the shape of a snake head and cut four heads out of green felt. Stitch two of the felt heads together with a running stitch along the edges. Glue on the underneath side of the squared end of the tie. Stitch the remaining two heads together along the curved edge. Stuff with cotton balls and sew closed. Glue wiggly eyes on top and glue to the top side of the squared end of the tie.

Tie the ribbon in a bow and glue on the top side at the point where the head meets the tie. Cut a long, forked tongue out of red felt and glue on the top side of the bottom portion of the snake head. Glue two small pieces of Velcro inside the snake head on top and bottom pieces to keep the mouth closed and the candy inside.

Stitch along the width of the tie about 12" from the snake head and fill with Dad's favorite candy *eggs*.

PAPER BAG DAD

Surprise your dad on Father's Day with a gift in a bag that looks just like him.

Paper gift bag (size that will fit gift)
Pink or flesh-colored card stock (for head)
Wiggly craft eyes
Pink pom-pom (for nose)
Craft hair or yarn
Dark pink blush (for cheeks)
Black and red permanent markers
Pipe cleaner, optional (for glasses)
Ribbon to match bag (1-1/2" to 2" wide and 7" long—
    depending on size of bag)

Choose a gift bag in your dad's favorite color. Use a bowl, plate or cup to trace a head on the pink or flesh-colored paper appropriate for the size of bag. Cut out the head. Cut out ears and glue onto the sides of head, then glue the head onto the bag, leaving enough room at the top for the hair.

Glue on the eyes and pom-pom nose. Replicate your dad's hairstyle with craft hair, the same color and texture as his. Glue hair onto head. Use small amounts of hair for eyebrows, mustache, beard and sideburns, if your dad has them. Use blush to make cheeks, and draw a mouth with the red marker. If your dad wears glasses, bend the pipe cleaner into glasses and glue on. Cut the ribbon in the shape of a tie and glue to the neck. Draw a collar with the black marker. Put gift in bag.

"One father is worth more than a hundred school masters."
— George Herbert

COUCH POTATO GIFT BAG

If your dad likes watching TV, he'll love this couch potato bag filled with his favorite treats.

1 yard brown burlap
Scissors
Thread
Cardboard
Acrylic paints and brushes or permanent markers
Assorted treats: pop, chips, candy, fruit, etc.
Television guide
1 yard red ribbon or raffia, 2″ wide (optional)

Cut a piece of burlap 36″ wide and 29″ long. Fold burlap in half crosswise (18″ x 29″). Sew side and bottom seams and turn. Hem or fray top edge.

Slide a piece of cardboard inside bag to prevent paint from bleeding through. About 11″ from the top of bag, write "U.S. No. 1 Dad" and "Couch Potato Treats." Then paint or draw a potato with arms, legs and face. In bottom left corner write "Loved by (fill in name)." In the bottom right corner write "20 lbs. of Hugs and Kisses."

Fill the bag with a 6-pack of Dad's favorite pop, some chips, candy bars, fruit, etc., and the current television guide. Tie the top closed with red ribbon or raffia.

TRUTHS ABOUT MY DAD

This is a nice chance to tell your dad all the things you appreciate about him.

Decorate a jar and place slips of paper inside which state complimentary "truths" about your dad, such as:

- Dad has a great lap for holding me.
- Dad is a good listener.
- Dad keeps our car running.
- Dad is terrific at washing the dishes.
- Dad is a great cook.
- Dad loves me.

"He shall turn the heart of the fathers to the children, and the heart of the children to their fathers."

— Old Testament, Malachi 4:6

Coupons for Dad

Give Dad coupons that he can redeem all year.

SHOE SHINE

Trace your dad's shoe print on colored posterboard. Use a paper punch to make holes for laces. Lace with yarn and tie a bow. Write on shoe "Good for One Free Shoe Shine."

YARD JOBS

Give Dad a pair of cotton garden gloves. Decorate them with acrylic or puff paints. Fill with Dad's favorite treats and coupons—"Good for Lawn Mowing," "Good for Weeding," "Good for Trimming," etc.

GONE FISHING

Cut a fish shape out of posterboard and decorate it with spinners, flies, swivels, etc. Write on the fish "Good for One Day of Fishing."

CAR WASH AND WAX

Place sponges, car wax, car air freshener, etc., in the middle of a chamois. Wrap it up and tie a ribbon at the top. Add a coupon that says "Good for One Free Car Wash and Wax."

BEAR HUGS

With a little help, even the youngest child can give Dad a gift. Cut out a teddy bear shape and have child decorate it with markers, crayons, and stickers. Write on it "Good for Free Bear Hugs."

WEED EATER

Tie a trowel and a hand weeder with ribbon. Include a coupon that says "Good for One Free Weeding Session in the Garden."

HOUSE REPAIR HELPER

Buy Dad a new hammer, screwdriver, or another tool he needs. Include a coupon that says "Good for 2 Hours' Help with Fix-it Project of Your Choice."

DISH WASHER

Tie a ribbon around a dishcloth or towel with a coupon that says "Good for Dish Washing."

JULY

July means hot weather has arrived and summer is in full swing. Kids are splashing in the water and looking for things to do. Long lazy days and warm evenings are just right for meals outside.

This month we put our patriotism on parade as we observe America's birthday. The Fourth of July is right up there with Christmas and Thanksgiving as a natural time for establishing family traditions with lasting impact. Plan time to have a whopper of a July Fourth celebration.

Dress up the house with red, white, and blue carnations, put a firecracker on the table, and don't forget to include Betsy Ross and Uncle Sam. From noisemakers to centerpieces, you'll find something to put the "pop" into July.

The symbols of Independence Day have their roots in the first celebrations of our country's freedom. Making simple and safe Fourth of July crafts with your children is a good way to remember the historical meaning of Independence Day and explore some American history together.

Whether you're planning a backyard barbecue or picnic in the park, you'll find great recipes for outdoor eating in this chapter. And don't forget to look back to Memorial Day and ahead to Labor Day for more barbecue ideas.

Then bang a drum, sing an anthem, march in a parade, let your heart swell with pride, and celebrate our great country!

Independence Day

On the Fourth of July we celebrate the day the American colonies declared their independence from England.

By 1774, the colonists were becoming increasingly frustrated with England because of their escalating taxes, yet they had no representation in England's Parliament. King George III sent troops to occupy the colonies and quell any discontent. For more than a year, Congress tried to resolve the problems with England without declaring war, but during the spring of 1776, sentiment rapidly grew in favor of independence. On June 7, Richard Henry Lee of Virginia introduced his famous resolution that "these United Colonies are, and of right ought to be, free and independent States." The Continental Congress appointed a committee of John Adams, Benjamin Franklin, Thomas Jefferson, Robert Livingston, and Roger Sherman to draw up a formal declaration of independence.

Jefferson was given the task of preparing the draft. The Declaration of Independence he wrote set forth the position of the American Revolutionaries with moving eloquence, supported by strong legal argument. Few of the ideas were new. Jefferson said his objective was "to place before mankind the common sense of the subject, in terms so plain and firm as to command their assent. . . ." The committee and Congress approved the document with few changes. As Richard Lee said: "the Thing in its nature is so good that no cookery can spoil the dish for the palates of freemen."

The unanimous Declaration of the thirteen united States of America was signed on July 4, 1776.

Fourth of July celebrations were popular right from the very start. Philadelphia celebrated Independence Day in 1777 with parades of soldiers, cannons firing, bonfires, fireworks, ringing bells, and candles in windows. Traditions of picnics, parades, and fireworks were firmly established by the early 1800s. Today, skies around the country are ablaze every July 4 as Americans celebrate Independence Day.

In CONGRESS, July 4, 1776.

The unanimous Declaration

of the thirteen united

States of America,

When in the Course of human events, it becomes necessary for one people to dissolve the political bands which have connected them with another, and to assume among the powers of the earth, the separate and equal station to which the Laws of Nature and of Nature's God entitle them, a decent respect to the opinions of mankind requires that they should declare the causes which impel them to the separation.——

We hold these truths to be self-evident, that all men are created equal, that they are endowed by their Creator with certain unalienable Rights, that among these are Life, Liberty and the pursuit of Happiness.——

That to secure these rights, Governments are instituted among Men, deriving their just powers from the consent of the governed,——

That whenever any Form of Government becomes destructive of these ends, it is the Right of the People to alter or to abolish it, and to institute new Government, laying its foundation on such principles and organizing its powers in such form, as to them shall seem most likely to effect their Safety and Happiness. . . .

And for the support of this Declaration, with a firm reliance on the protection of divine Providence, we mutually pledge to each other our Lives, our Fortunes and our sacred Honor.

Trill the fife and beat the drum— Independence Day is come!

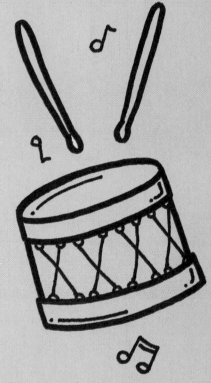

Thomas Jefferson was the author of the Declaration of Independence and John Adams was its strongest defender during the Congressional debate. Exactly 50 years after they signed that historical document, both Adams, our second president, and Jefferson, our third president, died on July 4, 1826! Adams was 90 years old and Jefferson was 83, which was very old for that time.

Watching fireworks brings out the patriotism in each of us. Put some fireworks into your Independence Day celebration with these sparkling decorations. Have a barbecue in the park and finish with a Star-Spangled Cake that will surprise your family or guests.

UNCLE SAM

Make a whimsical centerpiece from materials you have around the house.

3 rolls bathroom tissue (white)
1 roll bathroom tissue (pink)
Red masking tape
Posterboard (blue and pink)
Scissors
Small American flag
1 (14" x 7") piece of blue felt
Small foil star stickers (optional)
Glue gun
Small sponge
Pink paint
Puff paints or markers (black and red)
Cotton balls

Evenly space red tape around a roll of white tissue to make vertically striped pant legs. Cut a piece of blue posterboard in the shape of feet and glue it to the underside of the roll, allowing the feet to show.

Make the torso from a second roll of white tissue. To make a jacket, cut a piece of blue felt almost large enough to wrap around the roll, but leave a 1″ gap down the center for the jacket buttons. Fold back the top corners of the jacket to look like a lapel and glue the jacket to the tissue roll. Cut stars from the blue felt or use foil star stickers for the jacket buttons and glue them in place. Cut hands from the pink posterboard and arms from the blue posterboard, adding 1″ to the top of each arm to create a flap. Glue the flag to one hand and glue the hands to the arms. Bend down the 1″ flap at the top of each arm and use these flaps to glue the arms onto the top of the roll of tissue. Glue the torso to the legs.

The Liberty Bell, which hangs in Independence Hall in Philadelphia, is one of the most treasured symbols of American liberty. The inscription on the bell says in part: "Proclaim liberty throughout all the land." But nobody at the signing of the Declaration of Independence even mentioned the bell, and it wasn't rung until July 8. It didn't become known as the Liberty Bell until 1839, when the antislavery movement adopted the bell as a symbol of freedom.

Make the head from the roll of pink tissue. Very lightly sponge paint pink cheeks. Use black puff paint for the eyes and red for the mouth. Generously glue cotton balls to the head for hair, beard, and eyebrows. Glue the head to the torso.

Cut a circle of blue posterboard 2″ larger than the roll of tissue for the hat brim and glue to the top of the head. Use the last roll of white tissue for the hat. Evenly space vertical stripes of red tape around the top 2/3 of the roll. Make a hatband from a strip of blue felt cut wide enough to cover the bottom third and long enough to wrap around the roll. Carefully cut three stars in the front of the hatband, to allow the white tissue to show through. Glue the hatband around the tissue roll, with the seam in the back, and glue the hat on top of the head.

BETSY ROSS

Betsy Ross holds a small American flag in a tiny embroidery hoop!

Posterboard (blue and pink)
Bathroom tissue (1 roll each white, blue, and pink)
Scissors
1 (35″ x 6″) piece of red fabric
Thread
1-1/2 yards gathered red lace
2 yards (1/2″ wide) blue ribbon
Small flag
Tiny wooden embroidery hoop
Foil star stickers
Curly craft hair
Small sponge
Pink paint
Puff paints or markers (black and red)
1 (10″ diameter) circle of muslin
Cotton batting
Glue gun

Cut a piece of blue posterboard in the shape of feet and glue it to the underside of the roll of white tissue, allowing the feet to show. Sew the short sides of the fabric together and hem the bottom to a finished length of 5″. Gather along the top edge of the fabric to form the skirt and glue it on the top of the roll.

Glue the blue tissue roll on top of the white tissue roll, with the gathered edge of the skirt sandwiched in between. Cut two hands from the pink posterboard and two arms from the blue posterboard, adding 1″ at the top of each arm to create a flap. Glue the hands onto the arms. Bend down the 1″ flap at the top of each arm and use these flaps to glue the arms onto the top of the roll of tissue.

Form the bodice by crisscrossing red lace up and over the top of the roll to give the illusion of shoulders. Glue the blue ribbon to cover the edge of the lace. Tie a blue ribbon around the waist with a bow in front. Stick foil stars on the front of the bodice. Glue the small flag in the tiny embroidery hoop and glue to one of the hands.

For the head, glue curly craft hair on the sides and back of the roll of pink tissue. Place a small amount of hair across the front for bangs. Very lightly sponge paint the cheeks pink. Create the eyes and nose from black puff paint, and the mouth from red. Let the paint dry.

To make Betsy's hat, gather the edges of the muslin circle and stuff with cotton. Glue the lace around the top edge of the tissue roll and glue the muslin cap on top of the roll and lace, tucking the gathers underneath. Glue the head onto the body. Add a blue bow at the neck to finish.

LIFESAVERS FIRECRACKERS

This is a firecracker you can eat!

1 package Lifesavers, any flavor
Red tape, cloth or plastic
Small foil star stickers
7″–8″ silver pipe cleaner

Cover the roll of Lifesavers (except the ends) with red tape and randomly glue on foil stars. Insert the pipe cleaner into the center of the Lifesavers, leaving at least 2″ exposed for a wick. Glue two foil stars together back to back on the tip of the wick.

John Hancock was one of the most vocal critics of King George III's taxes. For his belligerence, the king put this founding father at the top of his list of most dangerous Americans. In order to annoy the king, John Hancock signed the Declaration of Independence "with a great flourish," and declared, "There, King George can read that without spectacles!" Because John Hancock wrote his signature so boldly and prominently, the term "John Hancock" has come to refer to a person's signature.

"POP-CRACKER"

This fun toy is much safer than a firecracker, and can be used over and over.

1 (3" x 4" x 1/2") scrap of wood for the base
Paint
1 (6-1/2") length of 3/4" wooden dowel
2 (3/4" to 1" long) wood screws
1 (1" x 1") piece of leather
1 (12") length of 1" PVC pipe
1 (1" diameter) cork
1 (18") length of metallic string
Decorative tape
Stars or holiday stickers
Metallic confetti (optional)

Paint the wooden base and let it dry. Using a drill bit that is slightly smaller in diameter than the screws, drill a hole in each end of the dowel and through the center of the wooden base. Screw the dowel onto the base.

Cut a circle of leather the exact size of the inside diameter of the PVC pipe. (It has to fit snugly so air can't get through.) Drill a hole for the screw in the center of the leather circle. Screw the leather onto the top of the dowel.

Decorate the PVC pipe with red, white, and blue tape, stars, flag stickers, etc. Thread the string through the cork and knot one end. Tie the other end tightly around the bottom of the dowel near the wooden base. Slide the PVC pipe down over the dowel.

Press the cork snugly in the top of the PVC pipe. As you pull the pipe up and push it down, the cork will pop out with a loud bang. (Don't pull the PVC pipe all the way off the dowel.) For a colorful explosion, pour metallic confetti into the PVC pipe before you put the cork in and . . . pop!

We would have had a turkey instead of an eagle as our national symbol if Benjamin Franklin had had his way. Franklin didn't like the idea of an eagle. He said eagles had "bad moral character" because they stole food from weaker birds. He favored the turkey because ". . . the turkey is in comparison a much more respectable bird, a true original native of America." Congress, however, selected the bald eagle, which is found only in North America.

UNCLE SAM NECKLACE

This easy-to-make necklace will delight younger children.

*1 old-fashioned wooden clothes peg (a clothespin with a wire
    spring won't work)*

Drill with 1/8″ (or smaller) bit

Acrylic paints (white, flesh-colored, blue)

Extra-fine-tip permanent markers or acrylic paints (red, black)

Paintbrush

Toothpick

Glue

Cotton ball

1 miniature black plastic hat, small enough to sit atop clothes peg

1 yard narrow ribbon or cord (blue or red)

2 blue barrel beads or blue pony beads

2 white round beads or white pony beads

2 red cartwheel beads

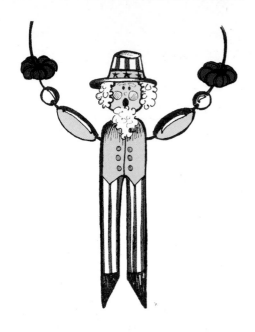

Drill a hole through the side of the clothes peg, 1/4″ below the head.
Paint the legs of the peg white and the head flesh color. When those
parts are dry, paint the middle section blue. Paint the lower 1/2″ of
the legs black for shoes. Draw red stripes on the white legs to resemble striped pants. Use the end of a brush or toothpick to dot the tiny
facial features. Mix white and red paint to make pink dots for cheeks
and nose. Draw black dots for eyes and a tiny red smile. Pull cotton
ball apart and glue small pieces on the head for the hair and beard.
Glue the hat on top of the head. Thread the ribbon through the hole
you drilled in the clothes peg. String one blue bead, one white bead,
and one red bead on each side of the clothes peg to make the arms.
Knot the ends of the ribbon together to complete the necklace.

(Note: If you can't find a plastic hat, make one out of felt or paint a
small wooden craft spool to look like Uncle Sam's hat.)

The History of "Uncle Sam"

Did you know there really was
an Uncle Sam? A man named
Samuel Wilson of Troy, New
York, supplied the United States
army with meat during the War
of 1812. The crates shipped to
the troops were marked "U.S."
Someone asked what the initials
stood for and was told, probably
as a joke, Uncle Sam, for Sam
Wilson.

The phrase caught on, and
soon soldiers were talking about
eating Uncle Sam's meat and
fighting Uncle Sam's war. Sam
Wilson probably didn't even
resemble the cartoon-like character drawn in the 19th century by
Thomas Nast, but in 1960, a
Congressional act declared Sam
Wilson the ancestor of America's
national symbol.

RED, WHITE, AND BLUE CARNATIONS

Turn some fragrant white carnations into a patriotic arrangement.

White carnations
Red and blue food coloring
2 clean pint jars
Florist greens or ferns
Vase

Fill jars 3/4 full of water. Put several drops of red food coloring in one of the jars and several drops of blue food coloring in the other. (The darker the food coloring, the more colorful the flowers will be.) Put the two jars side by side.

Beginning at the bottom and being careful not to break the stem, slice the stem of each carnation about halfway up. Put one side of each stem in the red water and the other side in the blue water. In about 4 to 5 hours the coloring will move up the stem, coloring the white carnations with red and blue streaks. Allow the carnations to stay in the colored water overnight for best results. Add florist greens and arrange in a vase.

FIRECRACKER CANDLE

It doesn't pop, but it looks like it's on fire!

1 (46 ounce) juice can (6"–7" tall, 3"– 4" in diameter)
Spray paint
Patriotic stickers
Styrofoam, 1" thick
9"–10" tapered candle
2 pounds dry ice
2 cups very hot water

Decorate the outside of the can in a Fourth of July motif with spray paint and stickers. Cut and fit a piece of Styrofoam into the bottom of the can. Press the candle into the middle of the Styrofoam. Drop small pieces of dry ice into the can around the edge of the candle. Add hot water and light the candle.

POCKET CHICKEN BREASTS

When cooking boneless chicken, allow 10 to 15 minutes per side. Avoid overcooking, but be sure chicken is cooked through and the juices run clear.

18 wooden (not colored!) toothpicks
3 tablespoons olive oil
2 tablespoons lime juice
1 tablespoon water
Cream Cheese Filling
6 skinless chicken breast halves

Soak the toothpicks in water. Combine olive oil, lime juice, and water in a small bowl. Prepare the Cream Cheese Filling.

Cut a horizontal slit in each chicken breast to make a 3″ square pocket. Insert 1 tablespoon of Cream Cheese Filling into each slit and fasten with the soaked toothpicks.

Grill the chicken over medium coals for 15 to 20 minutes, brushing occasionally with the oil mixture. Turn and grill for 15 to 20 minutes more, until chicken is tender and no longer pink. Serves 6.

CREAM CHEESE FILLING

2 cloves of garlic, minced
1 tablespoon snipped fresh chives
2 tablespoons snipped fresh basil leaves
1 (3 ounce) package low-fat cream cheese
Dash pepper

Combine all ingredients and mix thoroughly.

Barbecue Safety Tips

- Keep foods refrigerated until you're ready to cook them, including foods that are marinated.
- If you're precooking meat before grilling, immediately transfer it to the hot grill.
- When marinating raw meat or chicken, discard any leftover marinade. Don't use the leftover marinade as a sauce or save it for next time.
- Use a clean plate when you take your cooked meat off the grill, not the one that held the raw meat.
- When you're on outings, keep all meats, salads, and sauces in a cooler with plenty of ice.
- Promptly refrigerate any leftovers.

PILAF STUFFED PEPPERS

Try this as a main dish by adding some cooked chicken.

2 cups water
1 cup brown rice
1/4 cup bulgur
4 teaspoons instant chicken bouillon
1 tablespoon butter or margarine
1/8 teaspoon black pepper
1/2 cup chopped celery
1/2 cup shredded carrot
1/3 cup green onions, thinly sliced
2 tablespoons slivered almonds, finely chopped
3 medium green, red, and/or yellow sweet peppers
6 (12" x 12") squares of doubled heavy-duty foil
6 sprigs fresh parsley

In a medium saucepan, bring the water to a boil. Rinse the rice in cold water and drain. Add the rice, bulgur, bouillon, butter, and black pepper to the boiling water. Bring back to a boil, reduce the heat, cover, and simmer for about 25 minutes or until most of the water is absorbed. Stir in the celery, carrots, green onions, and almonds.

Meanwhile, cut the peppers in half lengthwise. Clean out the seeds and membrane. Place each pepper half, cut side up, on a piece of foil. Spoon the rice mixture into the peppers.

To make the foil packets, bring together two opposite sides of the foil and roll down toward the food in small folds. Flatten the two remaining foil ends and roll in toward the food in small folds. Completely enclose each pepper. Cook on the grill for 20 to 25 minutes or until the peppers are tender. Garnish each pepper with a sprig of fresh parsley. Serves 6.

Grilled Vegetables

Grilling raw vegetables intensifies their flavor, while giving them a slightly smoky taste. (Precooked vegetables tend to be mushy and less flavorful.) The intense heat quickly seals the outside of the vegetables, allowing the flesh to cook in its own natural moisture.

Scrub vegetables well with a brush, leave the peelings on, and cut to the desired size. When grilled, the skins become crisp and delicious. Brush the vegetables lightly with oil or marinade before grilling and place them directly over hot coals. After a minute or two, move them to the outside edges while you're cooking the main course.

Fresh vegetables may also be wrapped in foil packets and grilled. Tomatoes prepared this way are terrific when seasoned with fresh basil, shredded Parmesan cheese, and dry bread crumbs. Season small new potatoes with butter, thyme, and rosemary. Onion flowers are simple to make by cutting the onion into eight wedges, slicing the onions to within 1/2" of the base. Drizzle with butter and a little Dijon-style mustard, and sprinkle with brown sugar before wrapping in foil and grilling.

Most vegetables require 15 to 20 minutes on a covered grill, and 5 to 10 minutes longer for foil packets or an open grill.

FRUIT PIZZA

Pick your favorite fruit combinations or create a fresh version of "Old Glory."

1 (15 ounce) package sugar-cookie mix

1 (8 ounce) package low-fat cream cheese

2 tablespoons sour cream or yogurt

2 tablespoons powdered sugar

1 teaspoon grated lemon rind

1 tablespoon lemon juice

2 to 3 cups fresh or canned fruit, in any combination:

  Fresh or canned pineapple chunks

  Bananas

  Fresh orange slices

  Canned mandarin oranges

  Fresh strawberries

  Cherry pie filling

  Kiwifruit

  Grapes

  Peach or apricot slices

Preheat the oven to 350°F. Prepare the cookie dough according to package directions. Lightly grease a 12″ pizza pan. Press cookie dough into the pizza pan, about 1/8″ thick, and decoratively crimp the edges. Bake 8 to 10 minutes or until the edges begin to brown. Cool on a rack.

Combine the cream cheese, sour cream or yogurt, powdered sugar, lemon rind, and lemon juice and spread over the crust.

Arrange the fruit on top to create your own design. Serves 6 to 8.

(Note: Make a fruit pizza flag by pressing the dough into a 1/8″ thick rectangle on a cookie sheet. Use blueberries or blueberry pie filling for the blue field and strawberries or raspberries for the red stripes. Leave the cream cheese layer exposed in the appropriate places for white stripes.)

STAR-SPANGLED CAKE

Get ready for the "ooooh's" and "ahhhh's."

Chocolate bundt cake
1 (29 ounce) can cherry pie filling
1 small plastic cup
1 pound dry ice
Small tapered candles
Tiny flags
1 cup very hot water

Spoon the cherry pie filling on the top of the bundt cake. Place a small plastic cup in the center of the cake. Fill the cup with pieces of dry ice. Push candles and flags into the cake. Just before serving, light the candles and pour very hot water over the dry ice.

CUPCAKE-IN-AN-ORANGE

This is a crowd-size recipe, but it may be cut in half for a smaller group.

1 cake mix, prepared according to package
*   directions*
24 oranges
24 (12") squares of heavy-duty foil

Cut a 2" diameter slice from the top of each orange. Scoop out the orange fruit and pulp, leaving a clean shell. Save the scooped-out fruit for salad. Fill each orange shell 2/3 full of cake batter and place it in the center of a piece of foil. Replace the top of each orange. Bring the foil corners together at the top and twist to close. Place each package upright in the coals for 15–20 minutes. Serves 24.

(Note: These can also be placed on a cookie sheet and baked at 350°F for 15–20 minutes in a conventional oven.)

FROZEN *STARS & STRIPES* BARS

Layers of red, white, and blue make these frozen bars perfect for a hot Fourth of July afternoon, but experiment with different flavors for other summer days!

18 (8 ounce) wax-coated paper cups or plastic cups
18 plastic spoons (or new craft sticks)

BLUE LAYER

3 ice cubes and enough grape juice to make 1 cup
1 (3 ounce) package Berry Blue Jell-O
3/4 cup grape juice, boiling
2 cups frozen whipped topping
Blue food coloring

WHITE LAYER

1 cup vanilla yogurt
2 cups frozen whipped topping

RED LAYER

3 ice cubes and enough cran-raspberry juice to make 1 cup
1 (3 ounce) package Raspberry Jell-O
3/4 cup cran-raspberry juice, boiling
2 cups frozen whipped topping
Red food coloring

Put 3 ice cubes in a liquid measuring cup and add enough grape juice to equal 1 cup. Pour the blue gelatin into a medium-sized bowl and add 3/4 cup boiling grape juice. Stir until the gelatin is dissolved. Add the grape juice/ice cube mixture and stir until the ice cubes are melted. Fold in 2 cups of whipped topping. Add blue food coloring until the mixture is the desired shade. Spoon the mixture into the cups, filling each about 1/3 full. Place the cups in the freezer for about 30 minutes, or until the gelatin is firm enough to hold a spoon or stick. Stand a plastic spoon or stick in the center of each cup and freeze for another 30 minutes.

To make the white layer, stir the vanilla yogurt and 2 cups of whipped topping together. Spoon a layer of the yogurt mixture on top of the frozen blue layer and return to freezer for an hour.

For the red layer, prepare as for the blue layer, substituting cran-raspberry juice, raspberry gelatin, and red food coloring. Spoon into the cups and freeze for 2 to 3 hours, or until solid.

To serve, run cold water over the outsides of the cups to loosen. Makes 18 bars.

Try different juice and gelatin flavor combinations to make single flavor bars or bars with more than three layers. The ingredients for each layer will make six frozen dessert bars. You can also add miniature white marshmallows. If you're a yogurt fan, simply combine different flavors of tangy yogurt along with or instead of the frozen whipped topping! You still may want to add a bit of food coloring to make the colors vibrant.

AUGUST

There are no major holidays in August, so in between trips to the swimming pool, take some time to plan for the fall and winter holidays: Halloween, Thanksgiving, and Christmas.

Get a jump on Halloween costumes. You'll have plenty of time to plan and shop for materials. You might even start sewing! Make a written plan for your Thanksgiving menu and then smugly tuck it away in the November chapter.

Creating family holiday fun takes time and planning, so take advantage of the lull that August offers. Sit down with your family on a lazy day and ask them what Christmas activities are most meaningful to them. When they get used to the idea, they will probably tell you some interesting things. Take notes.

Many stores have end-of-summer sales, so start your Christmas shopping now. You'll appreciate your foresight during the Christmas rush. Picture yourself home wrapping presents and sipping eggnog with family and friends instead of standing in line on Christmas Eve. If you live near a Christmas tree farm, this might be a good time to pick out the perfect tree instead of tramping through the mud or snow in December. Just be sure to tag your tree and make yourself a good map!

You can always invent your own holidays. Turn your imagination loose and it will be easy to find reasons to revel. You might even want to get "National Stay Out of the Heat Day" on the calendar!

Although August has no *major* holidays, like every other month, it is chock-full of lesser known holidays and festivals. Numerous state and county fairs are also held during August. There are probably many interesting activities in your neck of the woods. Here is a list of events held throughout the world during August. The dates vary from year to year. Even if most of these functions are not within reach, this list should spark your imagination for your own activities to keep the summer doldrums away!

When it rains in August, it rains honey and wine.

FRIENDSHIP DAY   AUGUST 1

This is a day to heed the advice of 18th-century English philosopher Samuel Johnson, "A man should keep his friendships in constant repair." Sanctioned by Congress in 1935 for the first week in August, Friendship Day is an old observance deserving renewed attention, a time to acknowledge old friends and celebrate new ones.

ROUNDS RESOUNDING DAY   AUGUST 1

Sing rounds, catches, and canons in folk contrapuntal tradition.

INTERNATIONAL CLOWN WEEK   AUGUST 1-7

This day calls public attention to the charitable activities of clowns and the wholesome entertainment they provide.

NATIONAL SMILE WEEK   AUGUST 1-7

"Share a smile and it will come back to you, bringing happiness to you and the giver." (Sponsored by Heloise.)

NATIONAL CATFISH MONTH   AUGUST 1-31

Enjoy some Mississippi farm-raised catfish.

NATIONAL WATER QUALITY MONTH   AUGUST 1-31

Water is a precious resource. Research the importance of pure water to your body and find out about water quality in your area.

ROMANCE AWARENESS MONTH   AUGUST 1-31

This month was set aside to encourage couples to display romance throughout the year rather than just on Valentine's Day and anniversaries.

CHOCOLATE FESTIVAL AUGUST 2
Enjoy a day of chocolate meals, chocolate teas, and chocolate-eating contests like the folks of St. Stephen, New Brunswick, Canada.

MUNCHKINS OF OZ CONVENTION AUGUST 5
Wilmington, Delaware, celebrates Dorothy's arrival over the rainbow.

NATIONAL MUSTARD DAY AUGUST 5
Pay tribute to the condiment of kings—and the king of condiments.

TWINS DAY FESTIVAL AUGUST 5-7
Twins and others of multiple birth celebrate in Twinsburg, Ohio.

FAIRY TALE FESTIVAL AUGUST 6-7
Approximately 40,000 people see puppet shows, magicians, storytellers, and their favorite storybook and fairy tale characters in Lookout Mountain, Georgia. A similar festival is held simultaneously in Lookout Mountain, Tennessee.

LUMBERJACK FESTIVAL AUGUST 6-7
Try your hand at traditional lumberjack skills in East Meredith, New York.

GREAT CARDBOARD BOAT REGATTA AUGUST 7
Person-powered watercraft are designed, built of corrugated cardboard, and raced over a 200-yard course in Leon, Iowa. Have your own regatta, even if you have to float the boats in the bathtub!

HALFWAY POINT OF SUMMER AUGUST 7
At 10:33 p.m. EDT on August 7, 1994, 47 days, 1 hour, and 45 minutes had elapsed since the vernal equinox, and the same amount remained before the autumnal equinox. Do some research and figure out exactly when the halfway point hits this year!

SNEAK SOME ZUCCHINI ONTO
YOUR NEIGHBORS' PORCH NIGHT AUGUST 8
If you're a gardener, this one speaks for itself!

INTERTRIBAL INDIAN CEREMONIAL AUGUST 9-14
This major Indian festival in New Mexico brings more than 50 tribes together from the U.S. and Mexico. Similar events are held in many parts of the country to celebrate and preserve Native American cultures.

RIBFEST   AUGUST 11-13

During the second weekend of August, the smell of sizzling ribs tantalizes Kalamazoo, Michigan.

NATIONAL SCRABBLE CHAMPIONSHIP   AUGUST 11-18

The U.S. Scrabble championship is held in Los Angeles, California. This popular game was invented in 1931 by unemployed architect Alfred Butts.

INTERNATIONAL LEFTHANDERS DAY   AUGUST 13

This is a day to recognize the needs and frustrations of lefthanders and celebrate the good life of lefthandedness. Make the lefty in your house a VIP for the day and spend the entire day doing everything with the hand you don't usually use!

MIDDLE CHILDREN'S DAY   AUGUST 13

Middle-born children are always "too young or too old." Today they are JUST RIGHT!

NATIONAL HOBO CONVENTION   AUGUST 13

Even if you can't go to Britt, Iowa, for this convention, have your own hobo king and queen coronation ceremony, hobo parade, and Mulligan Stew.

OBON   AUGUST 13

According to Japanese Buddhist belief, the spirits of the dead return to visit their families every summer. Lanterns and huge bonfires are lit to guide the spirits home, and for three days families celebrate as though they're having a reunion with their relatives. On the last evening, they set out lanterns again to guide the spirits back. Those who live near water set lanterns on little boats, which gently float away. If there is a Japanese Garden near you that observes Obon, be sure to see this festival!

WORLD WHIMMY DIDDLE
COMPETITION   AUGUST 13

It's anyone's guess what a Gee Haw Whimmy Diddle Competition is, but 600 people get together for it in Asheville, North Carolina. Decide for yourself and try it!

What's Left Is Right

International Lefthanders Day was created on Friday the 13th of August, 1976! Superstitious people have long considered being lefthanded an abnormality. The Irish believed that lefthanders were friends of the leprechauns and fairies, but many traditions connect being lefthanded with bad luck.

Even our language does lefthanders a disservice. *Sinister* comes from a Latin word meaning "left." The French word for left is *gauche*, which we use to describe someone "lacking in social skills." The word "left" itself comes from the Old English word meaning "weak" or "worthless." Think about "two left feet" and "a lefthanded compliment!"

Many things in daily life are made to fit righthanded people. Scissors, watch stems, and golf clubs were all designed for righties. Redesigning things for lefties is not a new idea. In the 15th century, a Scots-Irish clan named Kerr (Gaelic for "left") had so many lefties in their family that they built their spiral staircase in reverse. Normally a staircase would spiral down clockwise, so that righthanders could effectively swing their swords to defend the upper floors.

LEITERSBURG PEACH FESTIVAL   AUGUST 13-14

Peaches are ripening this time of the year, and not just in Leitersburg, Maryland. Share a fresh bowl with your neighbors, make a peach pie, and preserve some for later.

FAMILY DAY   AUGUST 14

The second Sunday in August is set aside to focus attention on family solidarity and its potential as the best teacher of basic beliefs and values.

ROASTING EARS OF CORN FOOD FEST   AUGUST 14

The Museum of Indian Culture in Allentown, Pennsylvannia, hosts this traditional American Indian event.

NATIONAL RELAXATION DAY   AUGUST 15

Everyone should have a special day during the year for total relaxation.

NATIONAL AVIATION WEEK   AUGUST 15-21

Orville Wright's birthday provides a good reason to learn more about aviation. Visit an airport, design your own planes, go for a hot-air balloon ride, and learn how birds fly.

ANNIVERSARY OF ELVIS PRESLEY'S DEATH   AUGUST 16

One of America's most popular singers was pronounced dead on August 16, 1977, at the age of 42. Every August, admirers flock to Graceland, his home and gravesite at Memphis, Tennessee.

INTERNATIONAL FESTIVAL OF MUSIC   AUGUST 17

A classical music festival, considered to have the most spectacular scenery of any music festival in Europe, is held each year in Switzerland during August and September. Expose yourself to some good music.

ROCKHOUND ROUND-UP   AUGUST 18

Parrsboro, Nova Scotia, Canada, attracts 2,000 rockhounds for geological tours, workshops, and demonstrations.

**August brings the sheaves of corn.
Then the harvest home is borne.**

103

GREAT PIKES PEAK
COWBOY POETRY GATHERING   AUGUST 18-21

Check out a book on cowboy poetry (it's always entertaining!). Have your own Great Chow Down Barbecue, street dance, or pancake toss contest.

HOLZFEST   AUGUST 19

Woodcrafters of all types display and sell their products on the third weekend in August in Amana, Iowa. Look up *Holzfest* and make a wood project or try your hand at whittlin'.

DANISH FESTIVAL   AUGUST 19-20

The Danish heritage of the Greenville, Michigan, area is honored by 10,000 people each year. Learn more about Denmark or your own heritage.

BLACK HILLS STEAM AND
GAS THRESHING BEE   AUGUST 19-21

Each year the pioneer heritage of our country comes alive in Sturgis, South Dakota, with old steam and gas tractors, threshing machine demonstrations, flea markets, parades, antique automobiles, and dozens of other demonstrations related to yesteryear. Have your own milking contest with this comical Holstein made from foam core and a milk-filled surgical glove.

KISS-AND-MAKE-UP DAY   AUGUST 25

Here's a day to make amends and resuscitate any relationships that need to be revived!

BE KIND TO HUMANKIND WEEK   AUGUST 25-31

Make the world a nicer place, one person at a time! Sacrifice Our Wants for Others' Needs Sunday, Motorist Consideration Monday, Touch a Heart Tuesday, Willing to Lend a Hand Wednesday, Thoughtful Thursday, Forgive Your Foe Friday, Speak Kind Words Saturday.

The Anglo-Saxons called August *Weod Monath*, because it is the month when weeds and other plants grow most rapidly.

SEPTEMBER

By September, the sun rises a little later each morning and sets a little earlier each evening. The summer's over and fall is just around the corner. In fact, fall officially begins on the day of the autumnal equinox, sometime around September 22, when the sun crosses the equator, and day and night are of equal length everywhere in the world.

Fall is harvest time, when crops are gathered in and stored for the winter ahead. This month is the perfect time to make some autumn crafts which can be displayed through Halloween.

Labor Day may be the last big family get-together of the summer, so make it a special time of remembering. Put on a video or slide show of your summer vacation or hold a back-to-school fashion show for the kids as a season finale.

Usually the weather is still warm enough on Labor Day to have a great cookout. This chapter offers some unusual ways to make your outdoor cooking sizzle. Making your own barbecue from a clay flowerpot will delight your family and guests.

National Grandparents Day is a chance to do something special with or for your grandparents. A little planning can even bring you closer to grandparents who may be miles away. Make a phone call, plan a visit, write them a long letter, or do one of the activities described in this chapter. Don't forget those elderly folks in the neighborhood who may stand in for absent grandparents.

Labor Day

FIRST MONDAY IN SEPTEMBER

Early in our history, factories had very poor working conditions. People worked long hours for little pay in difficult circumstances. In the 1880s, labor unions were formed to try to improve working conditions and wages.

In 1882, Peter J. McGuire, a union leader in New York City, suggested a holiday to honor working people. The first Labor Day was celebrated on September 5, 1882. Ten thousand people marched in a giant parade in New York City and held a picnic afterward.

By 1893, thirty states were celebrating Labor Day on the first Monday in September. It became a national holiday in 1894. It is now a federal holiday and by separate legislation, it has also been made a legal holiday in each of the 50 states.

Labor Day is about midway between the Fourth of July and Thanksgiving, and everyone is ready for a three-day weekend. In many areas it's also the last day off before school starts. Organize some Labor Day fun with a picnic or barbecue and enjoy the last fresh fruits of the summer.

Fall fruits such as apples and pears have begun to ripen. It's a great time to lend an autumn touch to your decor. Make some delightful crafts and dishes with freshly harvested apples.

In 1898, Samuel Gompers, the pioneer who served as president of the American Federation of Labor for more than a quarter century, said this about Labor Day: "It is regarded as the day for which the toilers in past centuries looked forward, when their rights and their wrongs might be discussed, placed upon a higher plane of thought and feeling; that the workers of our day may not only lay down their tools of labor for a holiday, but upon which they may touch shoulders in marching phalanx and feel the stronger for it; meet at their parks, groves and grounds, and by appropriate speech, counsel with, and pledge to, each other that the coming year shall witness greater effort than the preceding in the grand struggle to make mankind free, true and noble."

HARVEST TIME GLOVE

The Little Crow would also make a good addition to your Halloween decorations.

1 cotton garden glove
Paint (recommended: American Acrylic Paints)
    Red (Country Red), Yellow (Cadmium Yellow),
    Orange (Pumpkin), Black (Ebony Black),
    Green (Evergreen), White (White Wash)
Paintbrushes
1 (3" x 5") piece of heavy cardboard
Cotton batting
Fall leaves, varied colors
Dried wheat grass
3 yards raffia
Little Crow
2 sunflower leaves, dried or silk
1 sunflower, dried or silk
Glue gun

Lightly sketch "Harvest Time" onto the front of the glove in pencil, then paint the letters in green. Draw two "patches" on the glove. Paint one red and the other orange, then outline them in black. Decorate the patches with green stripes and yellow dots.

Allowing the cardboard to extend 1″ above the glove, glue one side of the cardboard to the back inside of the glove. The cardboard will help hold all the things you glue inside the glove. Lightly stuff the fingers and palm with cotton batting.

Arrange the fall leaves, dried wheat grass, and Little Crow, and glue them to the cardboard. Loop a piece of raffia and tie it around the cuff of the glove. Glue on the sunflower and sunflower leaves.

LITTLE CROW

1 wooden egg, cut in half lengthwise
1 tongue depressor
Yellow felt or fun foam scrap
Paint (recommended: American Acrylics)
    Black (Ebony Black)
    Green (Bright Green)
    White (White Wash)
Black feathers
Glue gun

Glue a tongue depressor to the back, flat side of the egg, so that part of the tongue depressor hangs down below the egg and can be used to help hold the Little Crow in place. Paint the egg and tongue depressor black and allow them to dry. Cut a small triangle of felt or fun foam for the beak and glue on the round side of the egg, about 1/3 of the distance from the top.

Make eyes by dipping the end of a brush in white paint and dotting onto the egg. Allow to dry, then paint a small green dot in the center of the white dot. Let dry and finish with a small black dot for the pupil. Glue feathers on the back and sides of the egg.

> **"God sells us all things at the price of labor."**
> —**Leonardo da Vinci**

107

SCARECROW HAT

Hang this charming scarecrow on your wall, or add a wooden body and dress him for the porch.

1 large straw hat
1/2 of a straw hat, one size smaller than the large hat
Paint (recommended: American Acrylic Paints)
  Flesh-color (Flesh), Red (Country Red),
  Orange (Pumpkin), Black (Ebony Black),
  Blue (Country Blue), White (White Wash)
1" sponge brush
#8 flat brush
#1 liner brush
6 yards raffia
Dried wheat
8" piece of sturdy cardboard
3 yards colorful fall ribbon for a Florist Bow (see December)
3 sunflower leaves, dried or silk
1 sunflower, dried or silk
Dried wheat sprig
Clear varnish
Glue gun
Wire for hanging

Using the 1″ sponge brush, paint the crown of the larger hat (excluding the brim) flesh-color. Sketch a very faint black line from one side of the crown to the other, to mark the seamline down the middle of the scarecrow's face.

With the #8 flat brush, paint a red triangle on the center of the crown for the nose. For each eye, paint a heavy coat of white paint, then paint a blue circle and a black pupil, allowing each color to dry before applying the next.

Highlight the cheeks with dark pink by mixing red and white paint together and feathering lightly around the edges. Scuff an orange highlight onto the nose and cheeks with the sponge.

Draw black lines around the eyes and nose with a liner brush. Line a black mouth, and highlight the centers of the eyes with white. Paint black stitches on the nose and on the vertical seamline that extends from the forehead to the mouth.

TIP: Always allow time for each color of paint to dry completely before adding the next color. A hand-held blow dryer can really speed things up!

Hard work never killed a man, but it sure has scared a lot of them.

To make the hair, wrap raffia around an 8″ piece of heavy cardboard, slide it off, and wrap wire tightly around the middle. Cut the ends in several pieces and fray so that the hair looks scraggly. Glue the small half hat to the top of the head. Glue the hair underneath the brim of the hat, tucking the wire up so it doesn't show. Fray and fluff the raffia.

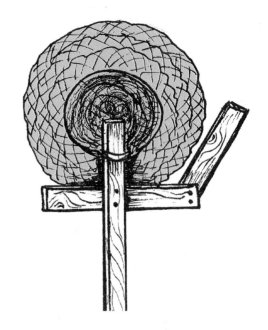

Glue wheat, sunflower leaves, and wheat sprigs on top of the hat. Make a small raffia bow and glue it to the bottom of the wheat. Glue the sunflower on top.

Make a bow with a few strands of raffia and secure it with wire at the chin. Cut some of the loops and fray. Make a Florist Bow and glue it at the chin, covering the top of the wire which attaches the raffia.

Protect the entire project with a spray of clear varnish and glue a wire to the back to hang.

SCARECROW BODY

1 (1″ x 2″ x 8′) board
Saw (to cut the board)
4 (1-1/2″ to 1-3/4″) wood screws
Flannel shirt
Overalls
Garden gloves
Newspaper
Raffia

Cut two 12″ lengths from the board, which leaves a 6′ section. Mark the center of one 12″ length of board. Attach it 6″ from the end of the 6′ board with two wood screws. For the raised arm, screw the second 12″ length to the end of the first 12″ board at an angle.

Dress the board in a flannel shirt and overalls. You can either put the long board through one leg of the overalls, or let the overall straps, placed over the shoulders, hold the pants up. Stuff the shirt, overalls, and gloves with newspaper. Tie the gloves to the end of the shirt-sleeves with raffia.

Attach the scarecrow face and hat by wrapping the hanging wire around the top of the board. Tie raffia around the neck. Lean the scarecrow against a bale of straw (in a sheltered area) or put him to work in your garden or front yard. If left outside, the scarecrow face will weather with time.

APPLE DOLL

This doll takes a while to make, but is a real treasure dressed in an old-fashioned outfit.

1 large Rome Beauty apple
Apple peeler (optional)
1 coat hanger
Wire cutters
Pliers
1 quart pretreating solution (optional—see Pretreating Fruit)
Knife
Food dehydrator (optional)
Acrylic paint
Paintbrushes
Spray varnish
2 straight pins with small black glass heads (for eyes)
Craft hair
Cloth body (available from craft stores that carry bodies for porcelain dolls)
Doll clothing or fabric scraps and lace

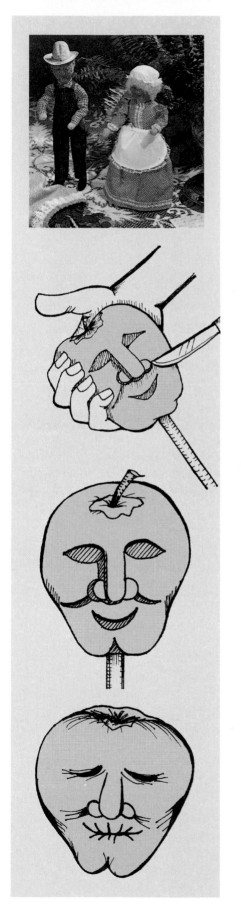

Peel the apple. Cut a 10″ piece from the hanger with the wire cutters and fold it in half with the pliers. Push the hanger into the bottom of the apple.

Part of the charm of an apple doll is the natural coloring that occurs as the apple dries. If you prefer the face to stay lighter in color, soak the peeled fresh apple in a pretreating solution for 15 minutes.

Create a face by carving around the features. Using the knife, lightly mark a triangle in the center of the apple for the nose. Slice away bits of apple from around the sides and bottom of the nose so that it sticks out. For the mouth, cut a wedge 1/2″ below the nose and cut two wedges for the eyes. Cut light lines in the forehead to make wrinkles. (All of the features will wrinkle as the apple dries and shrivels.) Soak the carved apple for another 10 minutes in the pretreating solution.

If you have a dehydrator, dry the carved pretreated apple for 24 to 48 hours at 150°F until the apple is dry, spongy, and wrinkled. (If you don't have a dehydrator, set the apple in a warm, dry place. Air drying can take from one to three weeks, depending on the temperature and humidity.)

When the apple head is completely dry, accent the facial features with acrylic paint. Spray the head with a clear varnish to prolong its life. Push the straight pin eyes into the carved eye sockets. Glue on the craft hair. Attach a cloth body to the hanger. Dress the doll in ready-made or hand-sewn clothes. A little lace around the neck hides the wire.

DRIED APPLE WREATH

Change the ribbon color to use this wreath for different seasons.

20 large firm apples
1 gallon pretreating solution (see Pretreating Fruit)
8 teaspoons cinnamon
4 teaspoons allspice
3 teaspoons ground cloves
3 teaspoons orrisroot powder (Orrisroot is a fixative, used to prolong the scent. It is also called Fiber Fix, and is available at craft stores.)
30" heavy-gauge wire or a (7" diameter) wire frame
Large plastic bowl with tight-fitting cover
Pliers
2 yards (1-1/2" wide) ribbon
12" thin floral wire

Peel (optional) and core (optional) apples and slice into 1/4" thick rings. Skins and cores left on the apples will give the completed wreath a different, yet equally attractive, look. Soak the apple slices in a pretreatment solution for 5 to 10 minutes. Drain and pat dry with paper towels. Combine cinnamon, allspice, cloves, and orrisroot powder in a covered plastic container. Place the apple slices in the container and shake to completely coat the slices.

Remove the apples and place them in a dehydrator, taking care not to overlap. (If you do not have a dehydrator, apples may be placed on screen trays in the sun. Cover each tray with nylon netting to protect the apples from insects. They will dry in 2 to 3 days. Bring them in at night or if it rains.) Dry until each slice is firm and has a spongy texture.

To make the wreath, shape the wire into a circle, heart, shamrock or other holiday shape, leaving the ends straight for threading. When using a purchased frame, straighten the ends with pliers. Fold apple slices into halves, then into quarters, and push the wire through each slice near the center.

When the wreath is as full as you want, bend the ends of the wire together with pliers. Make a Florist Bow (see December) and attach with thin floral wire.

Pretreating Fruit

If you want your dried fruit to stay light in color, before you dry it, soak it in a solution made from sodium bisulfite, lemon juice, or an ascorbic acid such as Ball 100% Natural Fruit Preserver.

Sodium bisulfite works best to preserve the color (and vitamins) in apples, pears, and peaches. It is a white salt, available from drug stores and winemaking supply stores. Dissolve 1 teaspoon in a quart of water.

Lemon juice and ascorbic acid do not work quite as well, but may be used. Dissolve 1-1/2 tablespoons of Fruit Preserver or 4 tablespoons of lemon juice in 1 quart of water.

Soak peeled or cut fruit for 5 to 15 minutes. Thinly sliced fruit requires less time.

FLOWERPOT GRILL

This fun barbecue is ideal for cooking on the balcony of an apartment.

Clay flowerpot, at least 11" high and 11" in diameter
Dirt or gravel
Heavy-duty aluminum foil
Charcoal briquets
Fluid charcoal starter
Small metal cake-cooling rack

Fill the flowerpot with dirt or gravel to within 5"–6" of the top. Cover the dirt with foil. Pile briquets on the center of the foil, apply charcoal starter, and light them. Place the rack on top of the pot.

Set the kabob ingredients in a row of plastic-lined flowerpots near the grill. Kabobs might include small cubes of tender beef or chicken, cherry tomatoes, mushrooms, small onions, green pepper chunks, zucchini, etc.

Have guests assemble their own kabobs. Provide sauces to baste the kabobs as they cook.

Fruit kabobs are a healthy summer dessert. Use pineapple chunks, maraschino cherries, banana chunks, orange sections, and peach slices. Brush with honey and heat for a few minutes on the grill.

Outdoor Serving Tips

The wheelbarrow and ironing board will remind everyone that it's a *labor* celebration.

- Hose out your wheelbarrow and spread a large sheet of plastic or garbage bags along the bottom and sides. Fill the wheelbarrow with ice and use it as an ice chest to keep soda, salad, watermelon, and other items cold for your Labor Day get-together.

- Use your ironing board as a serving table. Set up the ironing board and secure the legs with heavy bricks. Drape a festive outdoor cloth over the ironing board and load it with food, utensils, and napkins.

- Nest paper plates in appropriate-sized frisbees. The frisbees keep the plates rigid and easy to handle. When you're through eating, have a frisbee tournament!

BURGER KABOBS

Warm the pita breads on the edge of the barbecue. Slip the meatballs from the skewers into the pitas and top with condiments.

1-1/2 pounds extra-lean ground beef
1 small onion, finely chopped
1 egg, beaten
1/3 cup oatmeal
1/2 cup catsup
1/2 cup barbecue sauce
1 teaspoon Worcestershire sauce
4 pita breads, halved
Condiments (grated cheese, tomatoes, shredded lettuce, pickles, chopped cucumbers, mustard, catsup, etc.)

Combine all the ingredients except pita breads and condiments in a large bowl and mix well. Shape into 1″ meatballs and thread onto skewers. Cook on a greased grill over hot coals until well done. Remove the meatballs from skewers and place 2 to 3 meatballs in each pita half. Top with condiments. Serves 4 to 6.

WHEELBARROW DIRT DESSERT

This dessert maintains the *labor* theme.

Dirt Dessert (see May)
Clean child's wheelbarrow
Gummi worms

Make a triple recipe of Dirt Dessert and serve it with gummi worms in a clean child's wheelbarrow.

Grilling Tips

- Lightly coat your grill rack with vegetable oil or a nonstick cooking spray before placing it over the coals.
- To help prevent sticking, heat the rack for 5 to 10 minutes before setting the food on it.
- Either metal or bamboo skewers works fine. If you're using bamboo skewers, soak them in water for 30 minutes before threading.
- Put the foods that need to cook the longest, such as meat or raw vegetables, in the center of the skewer. Place tender items that cook quickly on the ends.
- Cook kabobs over a medium-hot fire. The coals should be gray with a red underglow.
- Turn the kabobs only once or twice with long-handled barbecue tongs or oven mitts.
- If you have trouble with food flopping to its heavy side when turning over, thread on two skewers.
- To minimize flare-ups, trim all the excess fat from the meat before grilling. Lowering the heat also reduces flare-ups. To reduce the heat, raise the grill, space the coals further apart, remove some of the coals, or reduce the fire's air supply by putting a cover on the barbecue or closing the air vents. If flames are beginning to burn the meat, remove the meat and mist the flames with a spray bottle, but don't soak the coals.

FLOWER BASKET BUFFET

**This edible centerpiece is a garden salad buffet
no one will forget.**

1 large (18" x 23") wicker flower basket
Plastic wrap
Paper towels
Florist's wire
Romaine or leaf lettuce and curly endive
Cauliflower and broccoli, cut into flowerets
2 large red cabbages, cut in wedges
Several large green peppers, with tops,
  seeds, and membranes removed
Carrot sticks
Radishes, mushrooms, cucumbers and
  tomatoes
Green onions
Flowerpots
Tape
Seed packets (optional)
Salad dressings
Assorted salad bar toppings (corn, peas,
  breadsticks, croutons, etc.)

Line a large wicker flower basket with plastic wrap and paper towels.
Prepare vegetables. Cover the bottom and outer edges of the basket
with lettuce and endive to make a green frame and backing. Arrange
the vegetables, starting at the back of the basket and working toward
the front. Tie groups of green onions to the basket handle with the
florist's wire.

Serve the vegetable basket with an assortment of salad bar toppings
and dressings in flowerpots lined with plastic wrap. Fold plastic wrap
over the edge of the pots and secure with tape. For a whimsical touch,
tape real or hand-made seed packets to the ends of servings spoons.

To serve, place several sharp knives and pairs of kitchen scissors
around the basket. Guests can snip off greens and trimmings onto
their own salad plates, and add other toppings and dressings.

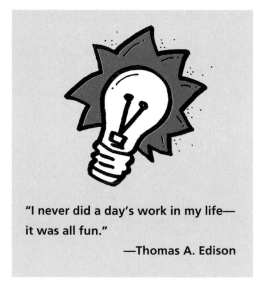

**"I never did a day's work in my life—
it was all fun."**

—Thomas A. Edison

APPLE DAPPLE CAKE

This raw apple cake is delicious and a snap to make.

4 cups apples, grated
2 tablespoons lemon juice
2 cups brown sugar, firmly packed
1/3 cup oil
3 egg whites
2 teaspoons vanilla
2 cups flour
2 teaspoons soda
1/2 teaspoon salt
2 teaspoons cinnamon
1 teaspoon freshly grated orange zest
3/4 cup walnuts, chopped
Powdered sugar

Preheat oven to 350°F. Grease and flour a 9″ x 13″ pan. In a large bowl, combine the apples, lemon juice, and sugar. In a medium bowl, mix oil, egg whites, and vanilla. In a large bowl, mix flour, soda, salt, cinnamon, and orange zest together. Stir the oil mixture into the apple mixture. Stir in dry ingredients and mix only until dry ingredients are moistened. Fold in walnuts. Pour into pan and bake for 35 to 45 minutes or until golden. When cool, sprinkle with powdered sugar.

Peter McGuire, the founder of Labor Day, was the son of Irish immigrants and had experienced for himself the extreme poverty that oppressed many laborers in the years following the Civil War. He went to work at the age of 11 and was employed in all kinds of menial jobs to support himself. According to a later recollection, he "was everything but a sword swallower. And sometimes I was so hungry, a sword — with mustard, of course — would have tasted fine."

Apples Aplenty

What is an apple? An apple is as old as Adam. It's what small boys shinny up trees after . . . and when one fell down on an Englishman's head several centuries ago, it led to Newton's law of gravity and a new age in science.

An apple is cider, sauce, butter, dumplings, pie, and pan dowdy . . . and about 70 calories. It tells Teacher she's "favorite" . . . and its blossoms tell poets, songwriters, and young lovers spring is here.

Apples get bartered for, begged for, and bobbed for . . . sliced, diced, peeled and "polished." They go into bushel baskets and picnic baskets . . . lunch boxes, sacks, and fruit stand racks. Apples get cooked, candied, and carameled . . . but mostly they're great for munching raw. They say apples keep the doctor away . . . and help bring kids in from play.

APPLEDOODLES

This is a modified version of old-fashioned Snickerdoodles and can also be made with dried pears.

Nonstick cooking spray
1/2 cup butter or margarine
1/2 cup shortening
1-1/2 cups sugar
3 egg whites
2-1/2 cups all-purpose flour
2 teaspoons cream of tartar
1/4 teaspoon salt
1/2 teaspoon cinnamon
1 cup chopped dried apples or pears

Preheat oven to 350°F. Lightly spray cookie sheets with a nonstick cooking spray and set aside. In a large bowl, cream butter or margarine and shortening with sugar. Add egg whites and beat well. In a medium bowl, mix flour, cream of tartar, salt, and cinnamon and add to creamed mixture. Stir in dried apples or pears. Mix well.

With your hands, form dough into 1″ balls and roll in the Cinnamon-Sugar Coating, covering completely. Place balls at least 2″ apart on prepared baking sheets. Bake in preheated oven for 7 to 8 minutes, until edges are slightly golden. Do not overbake. Cookies will puff up as they bake and look slightly underdone when removed from the oven. Remove from baking sheets and cool on a cooling rack. Makes about 5 dozen.

CINNAMON-SUGAR COATING

3 teaspoons cinnamon
1/4 cup sugar

In a wide, shallow bowl, mix the cinnamon and sugar.

"Man must work. That is certain as the sun. But he may work grudgingly or he may work gratefully; he may work as a man, or he may work as a machine. There is no work so rude that he may not exalt it; no work so impassive that he may not breathe a soul into it; no work so dull that he may not enliven it."

—Henry Giles

National Grandparents Day

In 1973, Marian McQuade wrote the governor of West Virginia and asked him to announce a special day for grandparents and their grandchildren. In 1978, Senator Jennings Randolph of West Virginia introduced a bill into Congress which designated the first Sunday after Labor Day as National Grandparents Day.

National Grandparents Day is a great day to visit your grandparents, write them a letter, or telephone them to let them know they are loved. Strengthening the special bond between grandparents and grandchildren enriches both generations.

TAKE YOUR GRANDPARENT TO SCHOOL

If you don't have a grandparent living nearby, adopt one!

Take your grandpa or grandma to school with you for a day. You may even be able to organize a *Grandparents Day* at your school. If you don't have a grandparent who lives close, adopt an older person in your neighborhood or church. These foster grandparents may not have their own grandchildren living nearby, or may not have any at all, and most will be thrilled to be included. Enriching relationships frequently result from young and old sharing and doing things together.

TREASURE ALBUM

This special scrapbook could also make a great Christmas present for a hard-to-buy-for grandparent.

Throughout the year, let children paste mementos such as artwork, outstanding school papers, photographs, and pressed flowers in a good-quality oversized scrapbook. Use rubber cement and photo corners for the best looking results, and have the children write appropriate comments on the pages.

GRANDPARENT MEMORIES

This gift will make your grandparents feel very loved year after year.

Create a special memory album for your grandparents. Using photos or magazine pictures, use each page to recount a memory of a special experience that you have shared with your grandparents. Write about such things as:

- "Remember the day we went fishing together?"
- "Remember the day you pulled my loose tooth?"
- "Remember our vacation at the beach?"
- "Remember the ice storm when we stayed at your house for four days?"

FAMILY PHOTO COLLECTION

Family photo albums help bond the generations together.

You know all the photos that are in a box in Grandma's closet? Spend a day with your grandparents and put all the photos in an album. Find out who the people are and label each picture with names, dates, and places.

Ask your grandparents to tell you stories about when they were young. Find out what exciting things happened during their lifetime. Record these stories in the album or preserve them on tape to listen to again.

Tape a Letter

Even young children who can't yet read and write can record a taped letter to Grandma and Grandpa. Have them start by talking about current family happenings and things that are important to them. For grandparents with a video player, let your child act out a favorite story or choreograph a dance. Little voices singing songs and telling stories will brighten the day of grandparents living far away.

FAMILY ART QUILT

Create a decorative, lasting family memory.

Fabric crayons
Typing paper
Muslin or other lightweight fabric (quilt blocks)
Border fabric, backing, and batting

Have everyone in the family make drawings on typing paper with fabric crayons. Any letters and numbers must be written backward so that they read correctly when held up in a mirror. Permanently transfer the drawing to muslin or another lightweight fabric following the directions on the fabric crayon package.

GRANDPARENT ACTIVITIES

Try some of the things your grandparents did when they were young!

- Have a potato-peeling contest to see who can make the longest strip.
- Play a game of marbles. Perhaps there's an old bag full of marbles somewhere in your grandparents' attic. A *taw* is a marble that you use to hit other marbles. There may be some *clearies*, *crystals*, *cat eyes*, *aggies*, or *steelies*. Draw a circle in the dirt or on the sidewalk. All the players put an even number of marbles in the center of the circle. Decide who will shoot first, and then go in turn. The object of the game is to knock the marbles out of the circle with your *taw*. You get to keep the marbles you knock out of the circle. The player with the most marbles wins.
- Visit a farm and milk a cow.
- See who can hammer a nail flat into a board the fastest.
- Have a clothes-hanging relay. Set up two clotheslines with clothespins and several baskets of clothes to see who can hang the most in the shortest time.
- Make butter. Put a pint of whipping cream in a quart jar, put the lid on tightly and shake the jar until a small ball of butter forms. Pour off the whey, add a little salt, and spread the butter on some warm bread or toast.
- Ask *your* grandparents for more suggestions!

"The harvest of old age is the memory and rich store of blessings laid up in earlier life."

—Cicero

I shall grow old, but never lose life's zest, because the road's last turn will be the best!

RAG DOLL

Make an authentic rag doll like your grandma played with when she was little.

1 yard natural muslin
3" Styrofoam ball (or wadded-up newspaper or foil)
2 small buttons (for eyes)
Acrylic paint, pale pink
Yarn or craft hair
Small straw hat or bonnet
Scraps of cotton print, lace, and ribbon (for apron)
Buttons, bows, and dried flowers
Glue

Tear the muslin into 1" strips across the grain, from selvage to selvage. Pull off any hanging threads and smooth the strips flat. Cut 9 strips of muslin in half and set them aside.

To make the head, place a strip of muslin over the ball so that the strip is centered. Leave the ends hanging down to form the doll's body. Cover the entire ball, criss-crossing the strips over the top, until you've used all but the short ones you set aside.

Tie the neck tightly with one of the short strips. Divide the body strips in half. Sandwich all but 3 of the short strips horizontally in between for arms. Tie the long body strips together under the arms with a short strip, making a waist. Tie one of the two remaining strips around each arm, about 1/2" from the end, to fashion the hands.

Glue on button eyes and daub on a little pink paint for blush on the cheeks. Glue the hair and bonnet or hat onto the head.

To make the apron, tear an 8" x 6" piece of cotton fabric. Gather along one of the long edges. Tear strips of fabric to make a sash and straps. Glue the straps across the shoulders and glue the apron to the waist.

Tie the sash around the waist and decorate with buttons, bows, and dried flowers.

(Note: Make a boy doll by separating the legs and tying them at the ankles. Make a pair of overalls out of an old pair of jeans and a fishing pole from a stick and string.)

> **Young folks ought to know that we old folks know more about being young than they know about being old.**

OCTOBER

October evenings are crisp and cool as thoughts of Indian Summer fade, but the days are alive with the vibrant colors of autumn. When nature's fall show is at its best, take the family for a ride to see the leaves and then come home to some hot apple cider.

Regardless of what this month might bring to mind for adults, to every school-aged child, October is synonymous with Halloween. For three months now, a favorite topic of conversation has been "what to dress up as" for Halloween.

Don't let all this high anticipation turn into stress for you. Let your hair down (maybe even dye it green) and get into the act. Wear a costume to work or the supermarket, and answer the door for your trick-or-treaters as a witch or Frankenstein. Get together with your neighbors and plan a party for the kids . . . or grown-ups.

In this chapter you'll find a score of simple ideas, including inexpensive Halloween costumes, great Halloween party themes, games, and yummy food for the little ghosts and goblins in your neighborhood. Put the decorations up early in the month and enjoy them until the werewolf howls on the 31st! As the Halloween makeup comes off, you can just hear it, "Next year I'm going to be . . ."

Halloween

OCTOBER 31

Most of the customs of Halloween are remnants of ancient beliefs. November 1 was New Year's Day for the Celtic tribes who inhabited Wales, Ireland, Scotland, and Brittany. On the preceding night, they celebrated the festival of "Samhain," Lord of the Dead, to mark the end of the harvest and the beginning of winter, the end of the old year and the beginning of the new. The Celts believed that during Samhain, witches and ghosts roamed the countryside and that the souls of the dead came home. They lit bonfires to scare away the witches and set out food and lanterns to welcome the dead souls.

The Roman harvest feast of *Pomona*, the fruit goddess, was held about the same time of year and the Roman conquerors added their own rituals to Samhain. The fruit centerpieces, apples, and nuts used in their celebration are still popular today. The ancient Romans also bobbed for apples and drank cider, traditions which are now part of our Halloween.

In the 800s, the Catholic Church declared November 1 as "All Saints Day" or "All Hallows Day." The evening before became "All Hallows Even," which was eventually shortened to "Halloween."

Although the mysticism of Halloween was not encouraged by the Church, people clung to the idea that dead souls were out and about on Halloween. In Ireland, if people went out after dark, they wore costumes and masks to frighten away the spirits and to keep from being recognized by the dead souls.

The Irish also originated the custom of "trick-or-treat" centuries ago when they went from house to house on Halloween to beg for food for a community feast and materials to make the bonfire. Those who gave generously were promised blessings for the coming year and the stingy threatened with plagues of bad luck. They also believed that the ghosts and witches created mischief on this night, so that any practical joke could be blamed on these supernatural forces. When the Irish Catholic immigrants began to settle in the United States in the 1800s, their Halloween holiday and many of its customs came with them.

Halloween today has only remnants of the ancient rituals. The ghosts and goblins and witches and black cats that had deep meanings in times past are now just part of the merrymaking, parties, and color of this holiday.

Halloween brings out the kid in everyone! It's just the excuse we've all been waiting for to dress up and be a little zany. Even workplaces are getting into the *spirit* of Halloween.

Let the kids show off their creativity and live in their imaginations. The sky's the limit! These ideas will make your Halloween a "spook-tacular" occasion!

PUMPKIN COSTUME FROM A GARBAGE BAG

This quick and easy costume takes only minutes to assemble!

Jack-o'-lantern garbage bag or leaf bag
Sealing or strapping tape
Drawstring
Stuffing material (newspapers, inflated balloons)
Green felt (optional)
Safety pins
Glue gun
Fall leaves (optional)
Headband (optional)
Elastic
Green, black, or brown sweat suit, or tights and leotard

Cut the bottom out of the garbage bag. Reinforce the cut edge with tape. Turn the top edge of the bag down 2″ and tape to make a casing. Cut a vertical slit in the casing and reinforce with tape. Thread the drawstring through the hole. Cut armholes on the sides of the bag and reinforce with tape.

Dress the child in sweat pants or tights so you won't have tape sticking to bare skin. Turn the bag inside out and upside down. Working on the wrong side of the bag (which is now turned to the outside), tape the bottom edge around the top of the child's legs, gathering as you go.

Turn the bag up, put the child's arms in the holes, stuff, and tighten the drawstring. Cut leaves out of green felt and attach them from the underside to the shoulders with safety pins.

Hot glue fall leaves to a headband or make a "stem" hat from green felt. For the stem, glue the felt into a cylindrical shape and attach an elastic chin strap.

Did you know that turnips were the first jack-o'-lanterns? Children in Europe carried turnips with them on Halloween night. When the first immigrants arrived in America, they discovered pumpkins, which were much larger and easier to carve than turnips!

CHRISTMAS TREE COSTUME

Twinkling Christmas tree lights make this costume sparkle.

2 (24" x 36") pieces of 3" foam
1 (36" x 36") piece of 1/2" foam
  (star and ornaments)
Green, red, and gold spray paint
Christmas tree decorations (garland,
  candy canes, etc.)
Contact cement
Battery-operated Christmas tree lights
  with a fanny pack (optional)
Green sweat suit or tights and leotard

Draw the tree design on the 3" foam and cut it out with an electric knife. Cut narrow, elongated slits in the body of the tree (don't cut all the way through) to give the effect of branches.

Make a large star from the 1/2" foam, and cut an oval in the center just large enough for the face. Cut round balls, bells, and other ornaments from 1/2" foam. Spray paint all the pieces.

Attach the ornaments to the tree with contact cement. Make small holes in the foam and insert the lights, running the wires on the back side to hide them. Attach the shoulder straps. Carry the battery pack for the lights in the fanny pack.

LIGHT BULB COSTUME

A glow-in-the-dark costume!

1 (36" x 36") piece of 1/2"–1" foam
Yellow or fluorescent yellow spray paint
Battery-operated Christmas tree lights (white or yellow bulbs)
  with a fanny pack
White T-shirt
Black acrylic or puff paint
Black leotard and tights

Draw the "light" design on the foam and cut it out with an electric knife. Cut an oval just large enough for the face and paint. Make small holes in the foam and insert the lights, running the wires on the back side. Carry the battery pack for the lights in the fanny pack. Paint "25 Watts" in black on the T-shirt.

Foam Costumes

Foam is available from fabric and home improvement stores, and makes excellent, lightweight, "sandwich-board" costumes. Adjust the size of the foam pieces to fit the person who'll be wearing the costume.

Cut the foam with an electric kitchen knife. Sculpt and soften the edges by angling the knife on its side. To give dimension to the pieces and make them look more realistic, vary the intensity of the paint, making some areas darker or lighter than others.

Be aware that some spray paints can dissolve the foam. Krylon brand is popular and does not cause this problem. Hot glue will also melt the foam. Use contact adhesive or contact cement.

To attach shoulder straps, make small holes about 1-1/2" from the edge of the foam. Thread cotton-webbing straps through the holes. Tie or glue them in place and reinforce with extra tape on the underside.

CHOCOLATE CHIP COOKIE COSTUME

This is a fun costume for the "cookie monster" in your house!

2 (24") circles of 1/2" foam
Golden-brown and dark-brown spray paint
1 yard (1-1/2" wide) cotton webbing (straps)
Brown stocking cap, and sweat suit or tights and leotard

Spray the foam circles with golden-brown paint and when dry, spray small spots of dark-brown paint to resemble chocolate chips. Attach the shoulder straps and wear over a brown outfit.

HAMBURGER COSTUME

No ketchup or mustard on this hamburger!

2 (24") circles of 2" foam (bun)
1 (24" x 24") square of 1/2" foam (cheese)
1 (20") circle of 1/2" foam (tomato)
1 roughly cut circle of 1/2" foam (lettuce)
Golden-brown, light-brown, red, yellow, and green spray paint
Contact cement
1 yard (1-1/2" wide) cotton webbing (straps)
Brown sweat suit, or tights and leotard

Paint the foam pieces appropriately. Paint small dots of light-brown paint on one of the bun halves for sesame seeds. Glue the lettuce, tomato, and cheese to the inside of the bun, allowing the edges to hang out. Attach the shoulder straps and wear over a brown outfit.

FRENCH FRIES COSTUME

Dress a sibling as a side order to go.

2 (36") squares of 1/2" foam (box)
10 to 15 (3" x 24") pieces of 3" foam (fries)
Golden-brown and red spray paint
Contact cement
1 yard (1-1/2" wide) cotton webbing (straps)
Red sweat suit, or tights and leotard

Add 12" to the wearer's shoulder width and 8" to the hip width. Cut two pieces of foam, the length of the torso and tapered from the shoulders to the hips. Paint the box red and the fries golden-brown. Glue the fries to the insides of the box, staggering their heights. Attach the shoulder straps and wear over a red outfit.

JAR OF JELLY BEANS COSTUME

This novel lightweight costume is comfortable for a small child.

Drawstring costume made of clear vinyl
Small, cylindrical balloons of various colors

Make a drawstring costume and stuff with inflated balloons.

BUBBLE BATH COSTUME

Bubbles, bubbles, everywhere!

20 to 30 round white, pink, or light
*   blue balloons*
20 to 30 safety pins
Pink sweat suit, or tights and leotard
1 barrette

Inflate and knot the balloons. Attach the knotted tips of the balloons with safety pins to the sweat suit or leotard and tights. Attach more balloons to a barrette with safety pins.

A BUNCH OF GRAPES COSTUME

Have a bunch of fun in this costume!

20 to 30 purple round balloons
Purple, brown, or green sweat suit,
*   or tights and leotard*
20 to 30 safety pins
1 yard green felt
2 to 3 yards green French-wired ribbon

Inflate and knot the ends of the balloons. Attach the tips to the sweat suit or leotard with safety pins. Put more balloons at the shoulders, tapering down to fewer balloons at the thighs to form a V-shaped cluster. Make a hat and leaves out of green felt. Add a twisted wired ribbon to form a curly vine.

Drawstring Costumes

Make a drawstring bag from a large piece of cloth or a sheet. Cut a long strip of cloth, twice the width of the wearer from elbow to elbow, and as long as the wearer's height from shoulder to knees.

With the right sides together, sew the two short ends together for the center back seam. Sew casings on the top and bottom. Put elastic drawstrings through the casings, leaving the ends exposed.

Try the sack on. Mark and cut a vertical slit in each side of the sack for the armholes. Turn the raw edges under and stitch in place or bind with bias tape. Put the bag on and cinch up the bottom drawstring. Stuff with wadded-up newspaper or balloons until the costume is round and full. (Balloons are more comfortable for the wearer, but give a bumpy effect.) Cinch the top closed.

In addition to the jar of jelly beans, this drawstring bag can be adapted for all kinds of costumes such as a jack-o'-lantern, tomato, or mouse.

SCARECROW COSTUME

You'll not only have a Halloween costume, but a keepsake of your child's face.

Petroleum jelly
Tissue paper
Plaster of Paris covered
 gauze (available from
 craft stores)
Water
Acrylic paint
1 yard elastic
Flannel shirt
Jeans
Raffia
1 (approx. 32" long) dowel
Straw hat
Garden gloves
Crow

Rub petroleum jelly on the person's face, lips, and eyebrows. Tie the hair back out of the way and cover the eyes with tissue paper. Dip pieces of plaster of Paris covered gauze into water and carefully apply them to the face. Leave large openings for the eyes, nostrils, and mouth.

Let the plaster dry for a few minutes and remove it (it hardens fast). Let it dry completely and then paint it with acrylic paints to look like a scarecrow face. Be creative in your painting!

Make small holes in the sides of the mask and attach elastic.

Dress the person in a flannel shirt and jeans. Use raffia to give the appearance of straw stuffing. Carry a dowel over the shoulders to rest the arms on. Add a straw hat, garden gloves, and a crow on the shoulder.

Although *pretending* to be frightened is part of the Halloween fun, some young children may *really* be frightened by masks and scary costumes. Reassure them by removing the mask and showing them that it is not real.

Halloween Superstitions

Halloween is a fun time to do some fortune telling.

- To see the face of your future spouse, stand in front of a mirror at midnight and look over your left shoulder, or look in a mirror as you hold up a candle.
- It is rumored that ghosts will write the name of the future intended in cornmeal placed by the side of children's beds.
- Superstition holds that if you look into the well at 11:00 a.m. on Halloween Day, your future will be disclosed to you.
- If a young woman places an egg in front of the fire and it sweats blood, she will succeed in getting the man she loves.

BATMAN COSTUME

Use fluorescent paint for the bat so that your little Batman is more visible.

Black sweat suit
1-1/2 yards (45" wide) black tricot
Small piece of heavyweight pellon
Large sponge
Fluorescent yellow paint
Needle and black thread
Scissors

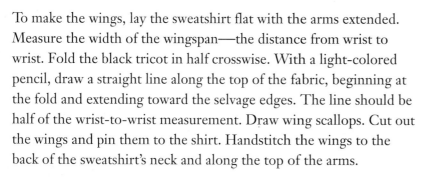

To make the wings, lay the sweatshirt flat with the arms extended. Measure the width of the wingspan—the distance from wrist to wrist. Fold the black tricot in half crosswise. With a light-colored pencil, draw a straight line along the top of the fabric, beginning at the fold and extending toward the selvage edges. The line should be half of the wrist-to-wrist measurement. Draw wing scallops. Cut out the wings and pin them to the shirt. Handstitch the wings to the back of the sweatshirt's neck and along the top of the arms.

Make a bat emblem on the front of the shirt by drawing a bat shape on the sponge and cutting it out. Dip the sponge in yellow paint and push it onto the front of the sweatshirt.

To make the headpiece, lay a large piece of paper on the table. Have the person you're making the costume for lay his head sideways on the paper. Outline his profile from the nose, over the top of the head, and down to the nape of the neck. (He can get up now!)

Allow a little extra for the seam as you draw a straight line across the bottom and extend it long enough to use for tying on the headpiece. Cut out the area for the mouth and chin. Cut two side pieces from the black tricot using this pattern.

Cut a 4" strip of black tricot for the center piece and four bat ears. Cut two ears from the heavyweight pellon. Stitch along the sides of the ears with the right sides together and the pellon on top. Trim the seams, then turn right-side out so the pellon is in the middle. Press flat.

Position one of the ears on top of the side piece where the ear should be, pin in place, and stitch. With the right sides together, stitch one side piece to the center piece. Repeat the process with the other ear and side piece. Turn the headpiece right-side out and cut holes for the eyes. Tie the headpiece on with the extensions.

WITCHES

People used to think that witches were people who worked magic and cast spells. They were evil because they were friendly with the devil. Halloween was their favorite night.

GHOULISH MAKEUP

Use fake fur, feathers, or cereal for ghastly special effects.

3 tablespoons cornstarch
1 tablespoon flour
3/4 cup white corn syrup
1/4 cup water
Food coloring
20 sheets (2 ply) facial tissue
Paintbrushes
Fake fur, feathers, elastic, cereal

Mix the cornstarch and flour together. Gradually stir in the corn syrup and water, and mix until smooth. Divide the mixture into small bowls or paper cups and add different food colorings to each batch of makeup. Leave one batch white for the base coat.

Separate the sheets of facial tissue and tear them into 2″ strips. Make sure that you have a good supply ready to apply quickly. Dip a small paintbrush into the white base and apply to the forehead. Put the tissue strips over the base coat and paint again. Repeat this process until you have covered all areas, except the area near the eyes.

Let the makeup dry for 15 to 30 minutes, then begin applying the colored makeup to desired areas. Several coats will intensify the color. By building up tissue strips, you can make cuts and scars.

To make a werewolf that looks as if hair is really growing right out of its skin, use small pieces of fake fur. Dip the ends into the makeup and apply the fur to the outside edge of the face, working in toward the nose. Apply several layers of fur to get a hairy look. Paint the nose with black or brown makeup.

For a bird disguise, use small feathers that can be found at craft stores. Dip the ends of the feathers into the makeup and apply them to the face, starting on the outer edge and working in. Add a beak made from paper or felt. Attach elastic and tie it at the back of head.

For a bumpy texture, mix different kinds of cereal in colored makeup and apply to the face. This makes a great dinosaur.

To remove makeup, splash the face with warm water and begin peeling off the layers. Rinse the face again with warm water and pat dry. Use a moisturizer afterward if your face feels dry. Dispose of makeup and tissue in the trash, not down the drain.

Ironing Board Ghost

This ghost can appear or disappear in a flash.

Stand an ironing board with the rounded end up. Drape or fasten a white sheet over the ironing board, forming a ghost. Cut eyes, nose, and mouth from black felt, and tape or pin them to the sheet where the face should be.

JACK-O'-LANTERN HOUSE

Is this eerie scene a HALLucination?

Large pumpkin with at least one wide, flat side
Sharp knife
Ice cream scoop
1 (24" x 24" x 1/2") piece of plywood covered
   with colored cellophane
Empty cardboard tube from paper towels
1 can to fit inside pumpkin
Broccoli
Leaf lettuce
Round toothpicks
Top of a fresh pineapple
Potatoes, carrots, and gumdrops (cars)
Round suckers, tissues, and ribbon or licorice (ghosts)
Dry ice

Position the pumpkin with the flat side as the front of the house. Cut the top off the pumpkin at an angle so that the lid will fit securely. Clean out the seeds and membranes with an ice cream scoop.

Near the middle and slightly up from the bottom, carefully cut out a rectangle for the door. Cut a square on each side of the door to make two windows. Remove the door and each window in whole pieces.

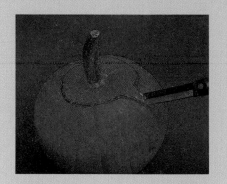

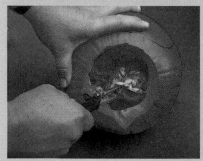

To line up a pumpkin lid more easily, cut a triangular notch on one side of the pumpkin lid as you remove it. It's easy to match the notch when replacing the lid.

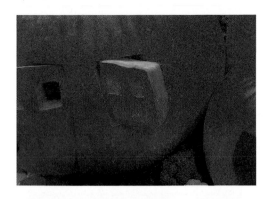

Trim the window and door pieces to about 1/2″ thick by carefully shaving the inside. Cut and remove individual windowpanes. Replace the windows in the pumpkin, allowing them to jut out ever so slightly. Position the door on the pumpkin as though it were just being opened.

Place the pumpkin on the plywood and the can in the bottom of the pumpkin. Use broccoli and lettuce leaves for shrubbery. To make the tree, stick several toothpicks into the bottom of the pineapple top, to stabilize it in the top of the paper towel roll. Wedge the tree securely between the pumpkins.

Make a car from the potato, using carrot slices for wheels and gum-drops for headlights. Make ghosts by tying facial tissue over round suckers with ribbon or black string licorice.

Just before your guests arrive, fill the can half full of hot water and add dry ice.

FRANKENSTEIN

This monster is a ghoulish centerpiece for your Monster Bash.

4 rolls bathroom tissue (2 peach, 2 white)

Puff paints or permanent markers (black and orange)

1 yard Halloween ribbon or fabric (patches, bow)

1 small plastic spider

Posterboard (black and pale peach)

1 (14" x 14") piece of orange felt (body)

Black raffia

Shredded metallic paper

2 silver pushpins

1/4 yard (1/8" wide) orange ribbon

Small craft pumpkin

Scissors

Glue gun

For the pants, glue the two rolls of peach toilet tissue together. Draw a line 1/2" from the top for a waist. Draw legs. Cut patches from the ribbon or fabric and glue them on the legs. Make stitches with black paint around the edges of the patches. Glue the plastic spider to one leg.

Cut a piece of black posterboard in the shape of feet and glue it to the underside of the roll, allowing the feet to show.

Glue a roll of white tissue to the peach tissue pants. To make a jacket, cut a piece of orange felt almost large enough to wrap around the roll, but leave a 1-1/2" gap down the center. Glue the jacket around the roll of tissue, matching the bottom of the felt to the bottom of the roll.

Cut hands from the pale peach posterboard and arms from the black posterboard, adding 1" to the top of each arm to create a flap. Glue the hands to the arms. Bend down the 1" flap at the top of each arm and use these flaps to glue the arms onto the top of the torso.

Cut 2 ears from the pale peach posterboard and glue to the tissue head. Draw Frankenstein's face, including grotesque stitching lines underneath his mouth and up the side of his face. Paint orange cheeks. Glue black raffia hair and a bunch of shredded metallic paper on the top of his head. Thread the 1/8" ribbon through the tiny craft pumpkin, fill the pumpkin with shredded metallic paper, and tie it to his hand.

Tie a bow tie from the Halloween ribbon or fabric and glue at the neck. Press the pushpins into the sides of his head underneath his ears.

BROOMS & BLACK CATS

Hundreds of years ago, people believed that brooms were the vehicles of witches and that brooms could work magic. Black cats were thought to be witches in disguise.

BEWITCHING WITCHES

Make a short fat witch and a tall skinny witch. . . .

*5 rolls bathroom tissue
    (pale green or white)*
*Posterboard (black and
    pale green)*
*1 yard Halloween fabric
    (for dresses)*
*Puff paints or permanent
    markers (black and orange)*
Black raffia
2 craft witch hats
1/2 yard (1/8" wide) ribbon
2 small craft pumpkins
Shredded metallic paper
1 yard (3/8" wide) orange ribbon
1/4 yard black nylon netting
Scissors
Glue gun

The
Phantom

For the tall witch, glue 2 rolls of toilet tissue together to make a body. Use 1 roll for the short witch's body.

For each witch, cut a piece of black posterboard in the shape of feet and glue it to the underside of the roll, allowing the feet to show.

To make a dress for the short witch, cut a piece of Halloween fabric 24" wide and 6" long. For the tall witch, cut the fabric 24" wide and 10-1/2" long.

Stitch a 1/2" hem in the bottom and a 1/2" hem in the top of each piece of dress fabric. Sew the short sides together. Run a gathering stitch on the long side, gather, and glue to the top of the body.

Cut hands from the pale green posterboard and arms from the black posterboard, adding 1" to the top of each arm to create a flap. Glue the hands to the arms. Bend down the 1" flap at the top of each arm and use these flaps to glue the arms onto the top of the torso.

On the remaining two tissue rolls, draw a face and paint orange cheeks. Glue black raffia hair and a witch hat to each head. Thread the 1/4" ribbon through each tiny craft pumpkin and fill the pumpkins with shredded metallic paper. Tie each pumpkin to a witch's hand. Tie ribbon or black netting at the neck.

Share the Spirit of Halloween

The Phantom will captivate your entire neighborhood!

Make two enlarged copies of the following message and *The Phantom*. Deliver them, along with treats, to two neighborhood doorsteps that do not have *The Phantom* posted.

If you do not wish a curse on this house, you must make 2 treats and deliver them to 2 homes in our neighborhood. You only have 2 days.

Post a copy of The Phantom on your door until Halloween to keep The Phantom from returning.

PAPER PLATE SKELETON

No bones about it! This is a cinch for little hands to make.

White paper plates
Paper punch
String
Paint or markers
Black construction paper
Scissors

Cut white paper plates according to the picture. To join the various parts of the skeleton, punch small holes at each point of contact and tie them together with string. Draw or paint features on the face. Accent the skeleton's scary face by cutting out eyes, nose, and mouth. Paste a sheet of black construction paper on the back of the plate so the paper shows through the holes. If both sides of the skeleton will show, attach an additional paper plate to form the back of the head. This skeleton is perfect for hanging in windows and on doors.

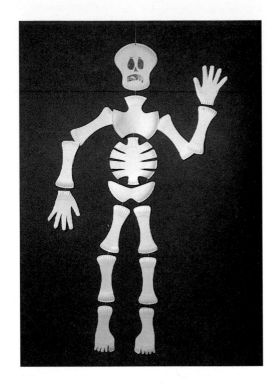

COAT HANGER BAT

Let some of these fellows hang around for some *haunted house* ambiance.

Wire coat hanger
Black plastic garbage bag (1 garbage bag will make 4 bats)
Black electrical tape
Newspaper or polyester batting
Reflective tape

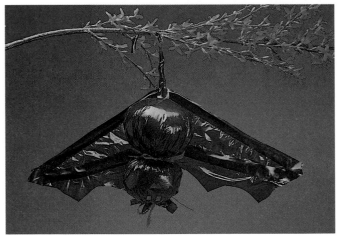

Bend the wire coat hanger to resemble bat wings. Lay the plastic garbage bag on a flat surface and place the hanger on top. Using black electrical tape, tape the hanger to the bag, leaving the hanger hook free. Cut the garbage bag around the edge of the hanger and form bat wings.

Cut an 18″ circle from the plastic garbage bag for the body and head. Wad batting or newspaper to make a ball about the size of a small fist. Place in the center of the plastic circle. Wrap the plastic around the ball and tape it to form the body. Make another ball of batting or newspaper and place on top of the body. Wind tape around the ball, forming the head. Cut ears from a portion of the leftover plastic bag.

Cut eyes, fangs, and wings from the reflective tape. Tape the body and head to the wings. Wrap black electrical tape around the hook.

BATS

During the Middle Ages, people linked bats with witches because they both came out at night and disappeared during the day. Bats also seemed mystical because they could fly at night and not bump into things. Now we know that bats have their own radar!

MONSTER BASH

Kids of all ages will have a monster-ously good time being, decorating, and eating monsters for the evening.

Try a variation on a traditional Halloween party this year. Let the kids make simple, scary party invitations . . . in monster shapes!

Have the children (or adults) come dressed as monsters! Play *The Monster Mash* and drape the house with crepe-paper cobwebs, black sheets, and creepy crawly creatures such as bats, snakes, and toads. Make some three-dimensional monsters to stand around looking scary. Let your imagination run wild.

Join us for a
Monster Bash
that happens to coincide with a goblin holiday! Festivities begin around _____ on _____ and continue until the goblins are driven away. Come costumed as your favorite Monster. The party is at

_____

Unknown prizes will be awarded for things we're not sure of.

Play a *Pin-the-Tail-on-the-Black-Cat* or *Pin-the-Nose-on-the-Witch* game, or have a treasure hunt. Hide caramels, plastic toy spiders and bats, gold candy coins, etc. in your yard. Give each player a flashlight to search for the treasure.

Make a pumpkin piñata. Blow up a large, round balloon and cover it with paste-soaked strips of newspaper. Let it dry for two days and then paint it orange and black. Pop the balloon and attach a wire for hanging. Fill the cavity with caramels and other treats. Hang the pumpkin up and let each guest take turns striking the piñata with a plastic bat. Watch the little monsters scramble as the treats come raining down!

Monster Cookies

Get everyone busy cutting and decorating Monster Cookies. Using the Santa Heart Cookies or Gingerbread recipes (see December), have children design and cut out their own Monster Cookies. Traditional cookie cutter shapes can become edible monsters with minor adaptations. Have several batches of Royal Icing (see April) or Buttercream Frosting (see December) available, tinted with wild and crazy colors, along with pastry bags and decorator tips.

GOBLIN GOLF

This modified version of miniature golf is a hoot for a Halloween party!

Several medium and large pumpkins
Carving knives
Acrylic paint
Krylon clear spray varnish
Posterboard
1 (1/4" x 10") dowel for each pumpkin
Glue
1 scorecard for each player
Golf clubs, preferably putters
Golf balls

Cut around the top of each pumpkin and remove the seeds and membranes. Carve the faces with the mouths flush to the floor or ground, so that a golf ball can roll in. Make small and large mouths to vary the difficulty of the course.

The eyes and nose could be painted with acrylic paint rather than carved out. Spray with a clear varnish after the acrylic paint is dry.

For each pumpkin, make double-sided posterboard "flags" in the shape of bats, witches, or ghosts. Label with "Hole #1," "Hole #2," etc. Glue the 2 sides together with the dowel in the middle. Push the flags into the tops of the pumpkins and arrange the course.

There are variations in how you can play and score the game. If you have lots of room, set a course with varying distances and difficulties. Determine a par for each hole. Make scorecards for each player, indicating par for each hole. The player with the lowest score wins. If space is limited, set up one pumpkin at a time and let each player have a turn. Score the same way.

Another option assigns higher point values to more difficult pumpkins. Any player who can get the ball into the pumpkin in one stroke (or set your own limit) gets the number of points assigned to that pumpkin, and the highest total score wins. Give the pumpkins as prizes.

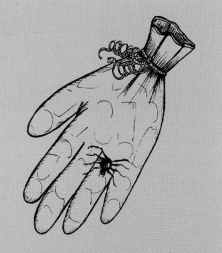

Monster Hand

Fill a surgical glove with candy or popcorn. Tie the wrist with orange or black curly paper ribbon. Add a spider ring and you'll have a scary favor for your Monster Bash or a "hand-out" for trick-or-treaters.

FLOATING HAND

This icy hand will give your guests a start!

Wash the inside of a surgical glove and fill it with water. Tie a knot or rubber band at the top. Freeze until solid. Carefully cut slits down the fingers and hand with a razor blade. Peel away the glove, being careful not to break off the fingers. Float the hand in very cold punch or put it wherever your imagination takes it. For an extra spooky effect, put dry ice in the punch, but be sure not to serve the dry ice.

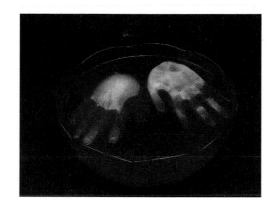

THE MUMMY WRAP

This is the funniest activity you'll ever do at a party. Everyone will be in hysterics!

Divide into teams of three and give each team three to four rolls of bathroom tissue. One person is the mummy and the other two wrap him up. Prizes can be awarded for the best wrapped mummy and for the fastest wrapped mummy.

CREEPY CRAWLY SPIDER RACE

This requires more coordination than you might think!

2 wiggly eyes
2 (1") orange pom-poms (eyes)
1 black paper plate for each spider
8 pipe cleaners (legs)
Hole punch
2 (12') lengths of string
Glue

Make 1 spider for each team of 2 players. Glue the wiggly eyes onto the pom-poms and the pom-poms onto the plate. Bend the pipe cleaners to make legs and glue them to the sides of the paper plate. Punch two holes in the plate and thread a string through each hole.

Have each team member hold the end of one string in each hand and stand 12' apart. Make the spider walk from one team member to the other by working the strings.

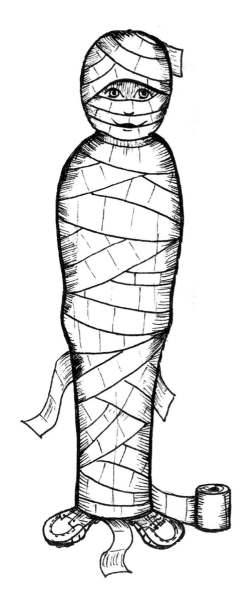

DRY ICE JACK-O'-LANTERN

This spook-tacular pumpkin can be friendly or scary.

Pumpkin
Knife
1 large can
Hot water
1/2 cup salt
Flashlight (optional)
3 to 5 pounds dry ice

Choose a pumpkin large enough to hold the can. Clean the seeds and membranes from the pumpkin and carve a friendly or frightening face. Fill the can about 3/4 full of hot water and mix in 1/2 cup salt. Place the can inside the pumpkin.

If there is room inside the pumpkin, place a flashlight between the pumpkin and the can to add to the effect. Wearing gloves to protect your hands, drop two or three large pieces of dry ice into the container of water. Dry ice will steam up and out of the eyes, nose, and mouth of the pumpkin.

As the water cools, ice will form around the dry ice, causing it to stop bubbling. Salt in the water helps to prolong the steaming action. After 15 to 20 minutes, drain the cold water from the container and replace it with hot water to start the steam again.

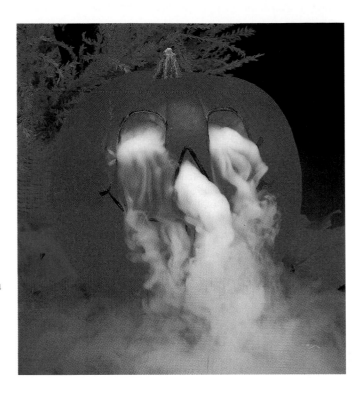

The jack-o'-lantern comes from an Irish legend about a fellow named Jack. One version has it that Jack lured the devil up a tree to fetch an apple, and then he cut the sign of the cross on the tree bark to keep the devil from coming down. Jack then forced the devil to promise that he would never claim Jack's soul.

When Jack died, he wasn't allowed into heaven because of his drunken and nasty ways. Seeking a place to go, Jack went to hell, but the devil made good on his promise and refused to let him in.

As Jack was walking away, the devil threw a hot coal from the fires of hell at him. Jack was eating a turnip at that moment and caught the hot coal with it. Ever since, Jack has wandered the earth carrying his turnip jack-o'-lantern, looking for a place to rest.

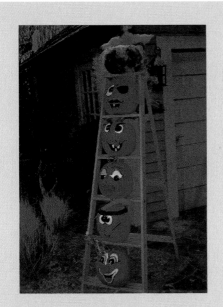

Jack-O'-Lantern Totem Pole

Stack decorated or carved pumpkins on each rung of a ladder. Add a little dry ice for extra spookiness.

CHOCOLATE GHOST PIE

No trick to make, but a real treat to eat!

Chocolate pie
Whipped topping
2 chocolate candies

Pipe whipped topping in a pressurized can or regular whipped cream in a pastry bag into the shape of a ghost on top of the pie. Fill in the outline with more whipped topping. Add 2 chocolate candies for the eyes.

FLAMING GHOST CAKE

Light up your party with this playful cake!

1 sheet cake
1 to 2 cups chocolate frosting
1 cup white frosting
Black string licorice
2 empty eggshells, halved and rinsed
2 sugar cubes
Lemon extract

Bake a sheet cake and frost with chocolate frosting. Make a ghost shape on the cake with white frosting. Outline the ghost shape with black string licorice. Place the clean empty eggshell halves, like small cups, where the eyes should be. Place a sugar cube that has been soaked in lemon extract into each shell. When ready to serve, light the sugar cubes, and turn off the lights.

Use permanent markers to decorate oranges with witch or jack-o'-lantern faces, and then hand them out for trick-or-treat or party favors.

Question: Which produce commodity sells the highest percentage of its annual supply in the shortest period? Cranberries? Apricots? Asparagus? Sweet cherries?

Answer: None of the above. The commodity in question has a 10-month season, yet sells 83% of its volume in one month. It is considered by many to be a vegetable, but it is a fruit. It is purchased by many customers, but eaten by few.

Give up? It's the pumpkin!

JACK-O'-LANTERN BUNDT CAKE

Use two bundt cakes to make this beguiling dessert.

3 regular cake mixes
2 identical bundt pans
1-1/2 cups orange frosting
3 ounces cream cheese (at room temperature)
3 cups powdered sugar
Green food coloring

Mix cake mixes according to package directions. Thoroughly grease and flour 2 bundt pans. Pour half the batter (1-1/2 cake mixes) into each of the bundt pans. Bake according to package directions. When the cakes are done, cool them in the pans for 10 minutes, then remove to a cooling rack and cool completely.

Trim the the flat side of each cake to make it level. Place one cake, flat-side up, on a plate and spread the flat side with a small amount of frosting. (Don't spread it to the edges where you could see it when the jack-o'-lantern is finished.) Putting the flat sides together and matching the ribs, lay the second cake on top of the frosted side of the cake to form a jack-o'-lantern. Pipe on orange-frosting features. Stuff the center hole with plastic wrap to just below the top.

Blend the cream cheese and slowly add the sugar while beating. When well blended, add a few drops of green food coloring. Mold into stem and leaf shapes. Set the stem and leaves into the top of the cake.

SPOOKY SPIDER CAKE

Decorating this cake is so easy that children can do it.

2 layer round cake
2 cups white frosting
1 cup chocolate frosting
Pastry bag with decorator tip
Toothpicks
2 small chocolate cake doughnuts (spider)
Pipe cleaners or licorice (spider legs)
Red hots, M&M's, and candy corn (facial features)

Frost your favorite cake white. Using the pastry bag, draw concentric circles of chocolate frosting on the cake. With a toothpick, draw lines out from the center, connecting the circles to make a spider web. Make a spider from the doughnuts, with pipe cleaner or licorice legs and a candy face. Place her on the web.

TOADS

Toads are associated with witches and witches' brew. People believed that toads were poisonous because animals that attacked them got sick. People also believed that toads can cause warts, which is not true.

GRAVEYARD CAKE

Make a haunting treat.

1 sheet cake
Chocolate frosting
Halloween candies
Fig Newtons (or flat square cookies)
Pastry bag with decorator tip
White and green frosting

Frost the sheet cake with chocolate frosting. For each grave, lay two cookies flat on the cake. At the head of each cookie grave, set another cookie at a 45° angle to form the headstone, propping it up with a bit of frosting and Halloween candy. Decorate or write on each headstone with white frosting, and make blades of grass around each grave with the green frosting.

SPOOK STICKS

Wrap white chocolate Spook Sticks in plastic and tie with a ribbon for party favors.

3 pounds white chocolate
Aluminum foil
Oil or vegetable spray
15 to 20 wooden ice cream sticks
40 miniature chocolate chips

Melt chocolate according to directions in the April chapter. Stir until smooth. Cover a baking sheet with foil and grease lightly. Dip the sticks into the melted chocolate until 2″ to 3″ are coated and place them on a baking sheet, about 4″ apart. (Vigorously stir melted chocolate each time you use it.) Pour the outline of the ghost with a small stream of melted chocolate and then fill it in. Before the ghost hardens, put two chocolate chips in place for the eyes. Refrigerate on baking sheets until chocolate is firm. Makes 15 to 20 ghosts.

141

DINNER IN A PUMPKIN

You can bake this tasty entrée inside a pumpkin.

1 small to medium pumpkin
Permanent markers or
*   acrylic paints*
2 pounds extra-lean
*   ground beef*
1 onion, chopped
2 tablespoons soy sauce
2 tablespoons brown sugar
1 (4 ounce) can sliced
*   mushrooms, drained*
1 (10-3/4 ounce) can cream of chicken soup
1-1/2 cups cooked rice
1 (8 ounce) can water chestnuts, drained and sliced

Cut the top off the pumpkin and thoroughly clean out the seeds and pulp. Paint a face on the front of the pumpkin with a permanent marker or acrylic paint.

In a large skillet, brown the meat in oil, and drain off the grease. Add onions and sauté until golden. Add soy sauce, brown sugar, mushrooms, and soup. Simmer for 10 minutes, stirring occasionally. Add the rice and water chestnuts, and heat. Spoon the mixture into the cleaned pumpkin shell. If you want to eat the pumpkin as a side dish, bake the stuffed pumpkin at 350°F for 1 to 1-1/2 hours, until the pumpkin is tender. Serves 6.

ROASTED PUMPKIN SEEDS

Roast the seeds from your jack-o'-lantern for a tasty snack.

2 cups pumpkin seeds
1 teaspoon Worcestershire sauce
3 tablespoons butter or margarine, melted
1 teaspoon salt

Rinse the pumpkin seeds until all the pulp and strings are washed off. In a medium bowl, combine the Worcestershire sauce, melted butter or margarine, and salt. Add the seeds and stir until they are coated. Spread on a baking sheet and bake at 225°F for 1 to 2 hours, until crisp. Stir frequently to prevent scorching. Makes 2 cups.

Cider in a Pumpkin

This jack-o'-lantern becomes a cauldron if you add dry ice!

Thoroughly clean the inside of the pumpkin, making sure you remove all the fibrous strings. Paint a jack-o'-lantern face with acrylic paints. Refrigerate the empty pumpkin until serving time. Pour cider into the cold pumpkin. Add dry ice for carbonation, but be sure to allow the dry ice to finish bubbling before you serve the punch.

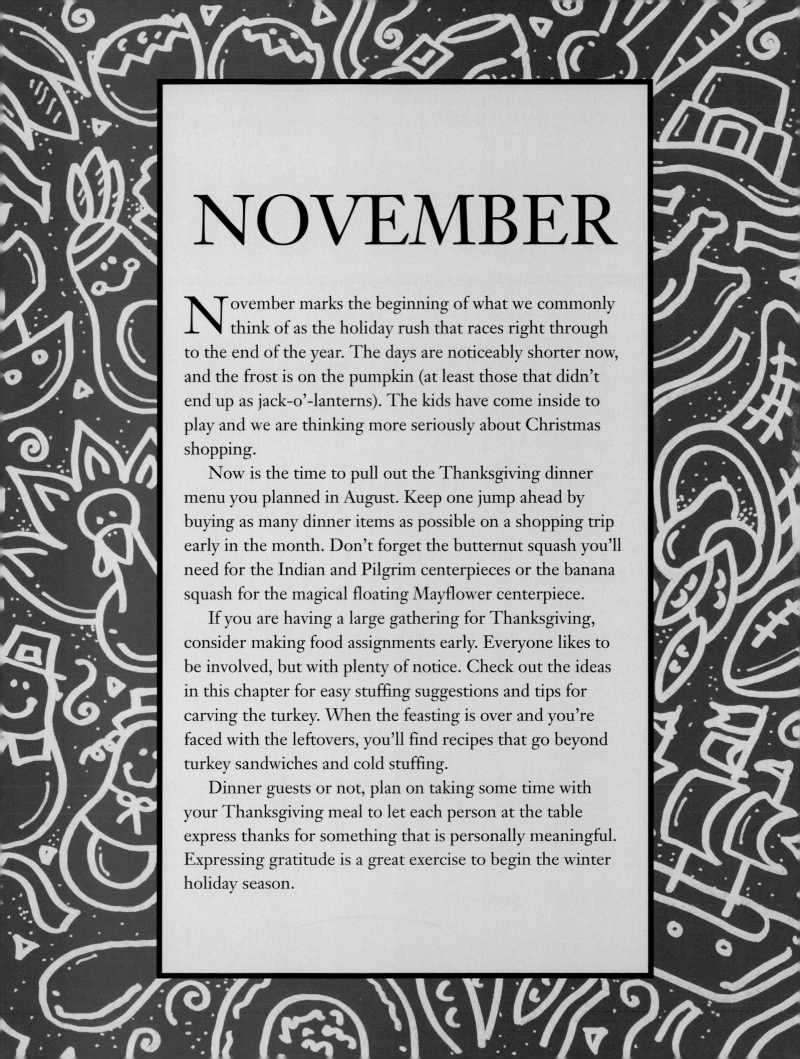

NOVEMBER

November marks the beginning of what we commonly think of as the holiday rush that races right through to the end of the year. The days are noticeably shorter now, and the frost is on the pumpkin (at least those that didn't end up as jack-o'-lanterns). The kids have come inside to play and we are thinking more seriously about Christmas shopping.

Now is the time to pull out the Thanksgiving dinner menu you planned in August. Keep one jump ahead by buying as many dinner items as possible on a shopping trip early in the month. Don't forget the butternut squash you'll need for the Indian and Pilgrim centerpieces or the banana squash for the magical floating Mayflower centerpiece.

If you are having a large gathering for Thanksgiving, consider making food assignments early. Everyone likes to be involved, but with plenty of notice. Check out the ideas in this chapter for easy stuffing suggestions and tips for carving the turkey. When the feasting is over and you're faced with the leftovers, you'll find recipes that go beyond turkey sandwiches and cold stuffing.

Dinner guests or not, plan on taking some time with your Thanksgiving meal to let each person at the table express thanks for something that is personally meaningful. Expressing gratitude is a great exercise to begin the winter holiday season.

Thanksgiving

There have been festivals associated with the harvest ever since man began to till the soil. The Chinese celebrated such a feast thousands of years ago, and in our hemisphere, Native Americans and colonists celebrated the harvest years before the Pilgrims arrived.

Nevertheless, Thanksgiving Day, as we now know it, traces its roots directly back to 1621 and the Pilgrims of Plymouth, Massachusetts. Persecuted in England for their religious beliefs, they sailed to Holland in hopes of finding a better life. Instead they found a language barrier, cultural differences, and economic hardships. Once again they uprooted their families, but this time it was for the promised freedom and prosperity of the New World.

The *Speedwell* sailed from Holland in July 1620, and met up with the *Mayflower* and more emigrants in Southampton. By the time they made it to Plymouth, England, the *Speedwell* had deteriorated so badly that it had to be left behind. Of the 102 passengers that sailed on the *Mayflower* that September, 41 were Puritans, who referred to themselves as "Saints"—17 men, 10 women, and 14 children. Eighteen were indentured servants, and the rest, called "Strangers" by the Puritans, were seeking economic opportunity, not religious freedom.

On November 10, land was sighted off Cape Cod. The Pilgrims chose a site on the mainland for colonization, and on December 11, first set foot in the deserted Indian town of Patuxet which would become Plymouth. (Three years of plague had exterminated the Indian population.) During a bleak winter filled with sickness and hardships, 47 members of the tiny community were buried in unmarked graves to prevent hostile Indians from knowing the number of dead.

The survivors' first harvest was a joyous occasion. A three-day festival of Thanksgiving replaced both Christmas and New Year's for these Puritan settlers. Their difficult living conditions left them little time or resources, and their religious beliefs also discouraged merrymaking, especially on traditional feast days which the established church had observed. Since God had allowed them to survive the winter, Thanksgiving seemed to them to be a more fitting celebration.

In 1789, George Washington proclaimed the first national day of Thanksgiving. Abraham Lincoln declared in 1863 that Thanksgiving Day be held annually on the last Thursday of November.

The American traditions of Thanksgiving are steeped in symbols of our first settlers. And don't forget your own family traditions, whether it's Aunt Nellie's candied yams or grandmother's china gravy boat. It just wouldn't be Thanksgiving without them.

PILGRIM AND INDIAN CENTERPIECES

Pilgrims and Indians bring to mind values our country was founded on: religious freedom, brotherhood, and hospitality.

1 butternut squash
Acrylic puff paints
1 yard narrow ribbon or braided trim
Craft doll hair
Small feathers
1 (14" x 14") square white felt
Black pilgrim hat
Straight pins
Glue

Cut a slice off the bottom of the squash to allow it to stand upright. Paint eyes and mouth on the narrow end of the squash. Add small dots of paint around the Indian's neck for beads. Paint designs or use braided trim around the wide portion of the squash. Allow to dry.

For the Indian, glue two braids of craft hair to a narrow decorative headband ribbon or braid. Tuck some small feathers under the headband. Glue or pin the headband and hair in place.

Adapt the Pilgrim patterns to fit the size of your squash. Cut pattern pieces from the white felt. Make pleats in the corners of the cap to shape it, and fold back 1/4" from the brim. Glue on the craft hair, cap, apron, and collars. Glue on a belt made from a narrow piece of ribbon. Using puff paint, add a gold belt buckle. Pin on the man's hat. Tie a small bow and glue it on the woman's neck.

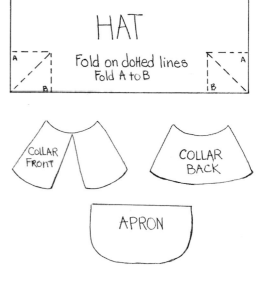

MAYFLOWER SQUASH

Dry ice lets this little *Mayflower* sail through the sea!

1 large banana squash
Puff paints or permanent markers
3 (4" x 3") pieces posterboard
3 (5" x 4") pieces posterboard
1 (6" x 5") piece posterboard
2 (1/4" x 11") dowels
1 (1/4" x 14") dowel
1 (8-1/2" x 11") piece construction paper
Glue
Blue cellophane
Several small clear plastic cups
Dry ice

Carve the squash as in the illustration and remove the top pieces. Scoop out the seeds and membranes.

Use puff paints or permanent markers to draw the windows and details on the *Mayflower*.

To make the flags, punch holes in opposite sides of the cut poster-board pieces and thread them on the dowels. Glue a small flag made from colored construction paper at the top of each dowel. Insert the dowels in the squash.

Fill the boat with raw cut vegetables and serve with a dip.

To make your *Mayflower* appear to be sailing on the ocean, scrunch blue cellophane around the squash and hide small clear plastic cups in the folds of the cellophane, 4"–5" apart. Place small chunks of dry ice in each cup. At serving time, pour hot water on the ice.

TURKEY PUMPKIN
Thaw frozen roll dough and roll 2 together, 1/4" thick. Form into breadsticks of various lengths. Make grooves for feathers. Brush with oil and let rise. Sprinkle with seasoning salt or Salad Supreme Seasoning before baking. Carve a turkey head from a yam. Add raisin eyes and an apple beak and wattle. Attach the breadstick feathers and the head to a pumpkin using bamboo skewers.

BREAD CORNUCOPIA

**This centerpiece is an interesting way to serve rolls at
your Thanksgiving feast.**

1 tablespoon yeast
3 tablespoons sugar
2 cups warm water
5 cups flour
1 teaspoon salt
Old fashioned V-shaped colander
Foil
Nonstick cooking spray
2 egg whites, slightly beaten
Pastry brush
Fall floral picks, leaves
Ribbon or raffia
Glue gun
Clear spray varnish

Sprinkle the yeast and sugar on the water and let them dissolve.
Gradually mix the flour and salt into the water mixture. Knead in a
mixer or by hand 5 to 8 minutes, until dough is smooth. Put in a
warm place and let raise until double in size, about 1 to 1-1/2 hours.

Cover the colander (or foil crumpled in a V-shape) and a cookie sheet
with foil and spray with a nonstick cooking spray. Roll out half of the
dough, large enough to wrap around and cover the colander. Brush
on slightly beaten egg whites to glue the seam edges together. Place
the seamed edge on the bottom and brush the dough with egg whites.

Roll out the other half of the dough and cut it into 1″ strips. Place
about 5 strips 1″ apart on the dough lengthwise from the opening to
the small end of the colander. Weave some of the remaining strips of
dough across the colander. Pinch the edges into the dough.

Twist the dough at the narrow end of the cornucopia to form a curve.
Roll back the extra dough around the opening or twist a strip of
dough and place it around the opening for a finished edge. Brush the
dough with egg white and bake immediately in a preheated oven at
400°F for about 10 minutes. Lower the oven temperature to 375°F
and bake for another 25 minutes, or until golden brown. If the cornucopia is getting too brown before it's done, cover it with foil.

TURKEY TURKEY SANDWICH
Use your leftover turkey in a *turkey*
sandwich. Make his tail with skewers containing cheese cubes, olives,
and cherry tomatoes.

Let the cornucopia cool about 5 to 10 minutes and remove the colander. Decorate it with fall floral picks, leaves, and ribbon or raffia. Fill
it with rolls. If you want to preserve your masterpiece for another
year, spray it with clear varnish and store in a cool, dry place.

YAM-STUFFED ORANGES

When the turkey comes out of the oven, the yams go in. When the turkey is ready to serve, the yams will be hot.

3 cups cooked, mashed yams or sweet potatoes

3 tablespoons butter or margarine

3 tablespoons orange juice

1/8 teaspoon salt

3 tablespoons apricot jam

1 cup miniature marshmallows

6 oranges

Preheat the oven to 325°F. Combine yams, butter, orange juice, salt, jam, and marshmallows. Decoratively cut the oranges in half and use a spoon to scoop out the fruit and pulp. Spoon the filling into the orange shells and arrange on a baking sheet. Bake 15 to 20 minutes or until the marshmallows melt and the yams are hot. Serves 6 to 8.

Turkey Carving Tips

Carving a turkey is a simple skill, and these few suggestions will help you carve your bird with ease.

- Slice the skin between the breast and leg.

- Continue to cut down to the joint, pulling the leg away from the bird while the tip of the knife severs the joint between the leg and the breast.

- Locate the joint between the thigh and leg with your knife and cut through the joint.

- Remove the large pieces of meat from the leg and thigh bones.

- Cut through the joint between the wing and the breast to separate the wing from the bird and cut the wing in half.

- Cut along the entire length of the breastbone with the tip of your knife. Remove the breast half by angling the blade of your knife and slicing along the line of the rib cage. You can also slice the breast without removing it from the bird.

- Thinly slice the breast across the grain of the meat.

One tale has it that the name *turkey* dates to Luis de Torres, the doctor on Columbus' first voyage, who exclaimed *"Tukki!"* when he first saw the unusual fowl. *Tukki* is Hebrew for "big bird."

TURKEY SALAD

Serve this versatile salad in pita bread halves or in a hollowed-out loaf of crusty French bread.

4 cups diced cooked turkey
1 cup thinly sliced celery
1 cup minced green pepper
1/2 cup finely chopped onion
1/2 to 3/4 cup low-fat mayonnaise
1 tablespoon lemon juice
1 teaspoon chicken bouillon granules
1/2 teaspoon salt
1/8 teaspoon pepper
Pita or French bread

GARNISHES

Almonds, toasted or
*   slivered*
Apples, sliced
Grapes
Pineapple chunks
Avocado slices
Hard-cooked eggs
Mandarin oranges or
*   sectioned fresh oranges*
Lettuce
Water chestnuts, sliced

Combine turkey, celery, green pepper, onion, mayonnaise, lemon juice, bouillon granules, salt, and pepper. Cover and refrigerate for 2 to 3 hours to allow the flavors to blend. Serve with the garnishes on a bed of crisp lettuce or in bread. Serves 6 to 8.

Double-Stuff the Turkey

If guests or family prefer different kinds of dressing, the bag method is especially handy. Stuff the neck cavity with one kind of dressing and the center cavity with another.

Unstuff the Turkey Instantly

Unstuffing the turkey is a cinch using this technique. The key is a cheesecloth bag which holds the stuffing inside the turkey.

To make the bag, cut a piece of cheesecloth large enough to cover the inside of the turkey cavity, with several inches left over. Stitch along two sides of the cloth to form a bag. Tuck the bag into the turkey with the unstitched edges hanging outside of the opening.

Spoon dressing into the bag until the cavity is loosely filled, then fold it closed and tuck the edges up into cavity. Secure the bag by folding the drumsticks under a wire holder or the thick skin that holds the legs together.

After the turkey is cooked, open the stuffing bag and spoon out enough dressing to allow you to grasp the edges of the bag. Pull the bag out of the turkey, dressing and all!

TURKEY DIVAN

This divine dish is so classy no one will think of it as leftovers!

1 (10 ounce) package frozen broccoli
6 to 8 slices of leftover turkey
1 (10-1/2 ounce) can condensed
    Cheddar-cheese soup
2 tablespoons milk
1/2 cup low-fat mayonnaise
1-1/2 teaspoons lemon juice
1/4 teaspoon curry powder
1 cup slivered almonds

Preheat oven to 350°F. Lightly spray a 2-quart casserole dish with vegetable spray. Arrange the broccoli over the bottom of the dish. Add a layer of sliced turkey. In a medium bowl, combine soup, milk, mayonnaise, lemon juice, and curry powder. Pour over the top of the turkey and sprinkle with slivered almonds. Bake the casserole 15 to 20 minutes. Serve with rice. Serves 4.

CRANBERRY RELISH

Brighten your dinner with this cheerful relish.

1 pound (4 cups) fresh cranberries
1-1/2 cups sugar
1/2 cup water
1/2 cup orange juice
Grated peel of 1 orange
1/2 cup finely chopped almonds, walnuts, or pecans
1/4 cup finely chopped celery

Rinse cranberries in a colander under cold running water. Discard any stems or shriveled cranberries. Place cranberries, sugar, water, and orange juice in a medium saucepan. Cook over medium heat, stirring occasionally, until skins begin to pop. Skim the foam from the surface. Stir in orange peel, nuts, and celery. Refrigerate until ready to serve. Makes about 4 cups.

Leftovers

Pour leftover gravy into muffin tins and freeze. Scoop leftover stuffing with an ice cream scoop onto a cookie sheet and quick freeze. Store the serving-sized portions in plastic freezer bags in the freezer.

Dressing Ring

Make some extra dressing to cook alongside your turkey or bake the next day to serve with leftovers. Press the dressing into a heavily greased ring-shaped mold and bake at 350°F for 45 minutes to 1 hour, until the dressing turns a light golden brown. Invert the dressing onto a platter. Fill the center ring with cranberry relish and garnish with carrot curls. Serve with leftover turkey and gravy.

DECEMBER

December is the crowning jewel of the year! Holiday music, lights, and tinsel twinkle in the cold night air. Wreaths and red bows adorn front doors and the calendar is crammed with a flurry of activities. Children and adults look forward to this magic time of year more than any other as we're celebrating Christmas and Hanukkah. All of our good intentions and goodwill are focused on this culminating season.

This is the month to revel in the festive atmosphere, and it needn't cost a lot. Take time with your family early in the month to plan your Christmas or Hanukkah as you fill out the Holiday Planning Calendar and make decisions about what you can realistically do in one holiday season. Block time for activities that get everyone into the spirit of the season like caroling in Reindeer Antlers. You could spread the spirit of the season throughout your neighborhood with a modified version of The Phantom (see October). In with all the company parties and shopping trips, plan time for projects that involve the whole family, such as the Family Tree Wall Hanging or one of the Christmas Memory Makers. You may want to bake some Santa Heart Cookies and dress them up in a Reindeer Gift Bag for a special neighbor.

Remember, making holiday memories doesn't require complicated activities. The ideas in this chapter are easy and meant to simplify an inherently busy time.

Hanukkah

Hanukkah (or Chanukah) is a Jewish festival, beginning on the twenty-fifth day of Kislev, the third month of the Jewish lunar calendar, usually in December. Hanukkah marks the reconsecration of the Temple in Jerusalem after its recapture from the Syrian Greeks around 165 B.C. A miracle recorded in the Talmud accounts for festivities held over eight days and nights.

During the Syrian occupation, King Antiochus IV decreed that the Temple of Jerusalem was to become a temple of the Greek god Zeus. He burned the scrolls of the Torah and attempted to force the Jews to make sacrifices to Zeus. Mattathias Maccabee and his five sons led a three-year-long revolt that drove the Syrians out. The desecrated temple was cleansed from top to bottom, a new altar was built of stones, and the traditional order of worship was restored.

To rekindle the flame of the Eternal Light, only one day's worth of pure olive oil could be found and it would be eight days until fresh jars of oil could be brought into the temple. Miraculously, the single day's supply burned for eight days and eight nights.

To remember this miracle, Jews light candles each night of the festival. The first evening only one candle is lit, the second night two are lit, and so on for the eight days. Hanukkah is also known as the Festival of Light, the Feast of Dedication, or the Feast of the Maccabees.

Sometimes gifts are part of the festival that celebrates the Jews' independence from their oppressors. Traditionally, Hanukkah gelt (money) was given, symbolizing the Jews' freedom to coin their own money. Today, in place of gelt, the gifts may be coins or chocolate coins wrapped in gold foil paper.

In some families, parents hide a gift for each child every night and the children search through the house for them. The gifts are often small symbolic tokens related to Hanukkah, such as candles, a menorah, a dreidel (a spinning top used in a children's game of chance), or cookies in Hanukkah shapes, until the last night when each child receives a special present.

On December nights, one can see flickering candles set in eight-branched candelabra through the windows of Jewish homes. The lights may be pale in comparison to the blaze of Christmas trees, but they symbolize joy, religious freedom, and faith. Hanukkah is a time for songs, stories, presents, riddles, arithmetic problems, games, prayers, and meals that feature latkes.

SANDWICH MENORAH

This snack is a reminder of the Hanukkah menorah.

1 large slice of bread
1/4 cup cream cheese, softened
9 pretzel sticks
9 candy corns

Spread cream cheese on the bread. Break a small piece (1″ or so) from a pretzel. Place the shortened pretzel in the center of the sandwich and the remaining pretzels on both sides of the smaller pretzel. Stick a candy corn at the top of each pretzel to represent the candles.

LATKES

Serve latkes with applesauce and sour cream.

6 medium-sized potatoes
1 medium-sized onion, peeled
1 teaspoon seasoning salt
1/4 teaspoon pepper
3 tablespoons flour
2 eggs, slightly beaten
1 to 2 tablespoons vegetable or olive oil

Peel the potatoes, holding them in cold water until they're all peeled. Drain on paper towels. Using a large grater or food processor, grate the potatoes and onion. Pour off any excess liquid. Mix the salt, pepper, and flour together. Stir into the potato mixture and mix well. Stir the eggs into the potato mixture.

Heat the oil in a large nonstick frying pan. Put two tablespoons of the potato mixture into the pan and press it into a thin pancake with a slotted pancake turner. Repeat until the pan is filled. Cook until each latke is golden brown, turn, and cook until the other side is golden. Keep warm in a 250°F oven until ready to serve. Makes 24 latkes.

The *menorah*, or candlestick, has become the central symbol of Hanukkah. With nine holders, there is a place for each night's candle plus one for the *shammash*, the candle used to light the others. In Hebrew, shammash refers to the servant. The shammash is lit first and then is used to light the others. When all the candles are burning, the shammash is put in its holder, which is positioned either higher or lower than the other candles.

The menorah is set in the window or another prominent place so that all may see it and be reminded of the miracle of Hanukkah. The eight candles represent faith, freedom, courage, love, charity, integrity, knowledge, and peace.

Latke is the Yiddish word for pancake. The Spanish explorer Pizarro brought potatoes to Europe from South America in the 1500s. The Jews living in Eastern Europe began using this common food as part of their Hanukkah traditions in the 1600s, and now it is part of the celebration worldwide.

Christmas

Christmas celebrates the birth of Jesus Christ, although it has never been seriously claimed that December 25 was his true birthday. Before the fourth century, it was celebrated in April or May, which more closely matches the scriptural account.

As Christian festivals were substituted for pagan ones, the winter solstice festivities of light and rebirth seemed a natural time to celebrate Jesus' birth. Through the centuries, folk customs celebrating the coming of longer days were combined with church observances celebrating the "Sun of Righteousness." Christmas today is the sum of customs observed for so long that their origins may have been forgotten.

The Roman tradition of giving New Year's gifts continued well into the Middle Ages, but in the 12th century, the tradition of giving gifts for Christmas began, inspired by the account of the wise men, who brought gifts to the Christ Child. In English commonwealth countries, Boxing Day is the first weekday following Christmas. The name comes from the boxed presents given to servants and other helpful folks like the postman and trash collector.

In Sweden, children have their gifts and tree on Christmas Eve. Sometimes gifts are thrown in the front door by mysterious donors who quickly run away. In Norway, gifts may be hidden away in different parts of the house for the children to find. In both of these countries, sheaves of grain are put out on rooftops or hung on poles, so that the birds may also enjoy a Christmas dinner.

The custom of decorating the tree comes from Germany. Although trees may have been part of a pagan festival, many people believe it was Martin Luther who thought of decorating the first Christmas tree.

In Italy, a little old woman named *Befana* is believed to come and leave delightful gifts in the stockings of good children while she leaves birch rods or charcoal ashes for those who are bad. In Holland and Belgium, St. Nicholas, dressed in magnificent robes, comes riding on a horse and inquires about the behavior of the children. Children with good reports find their shoes full of gifts in the morning, while naughty children find birch rods.

The American *Santa Claus* was adapted from the Dutch *Saint Nikolas* when they settled in New Amsterdam. Most of the Santa legend, such as his climb down the chimney and his red suit, are of Dutch origin. His reindeer and the North Pole, however, came from Scandinavia.

Take some time this year to discover the meaning of your Christmas traditions and start a new tradition or two. New traditions can deepen our appreciation for the universal nature of holiday observances, especially at this time when the central theme of the season is peace on earth, goodwill toward all men.

There are more ways to celebrate Christmas than you can count. The ideas in this chapter are easy and fun and can be used to involve little hands. Pick and choose a few that will enhance your Christmas and put a smile on someone's face.

HOLIDAY PLANNING CALENDAR

Planning makes perfect!

Large appointment or desk pad calendar
Christmas stickers
Colored markers

At the beginning of the holiday season, set aside a special family night for planning. Write in shopping trips with smaller children, parties, Christmas concerts, the day for tree selection and trimming, Christmas gift wrapping, and baking. Scheduling your time and energy takes a lot of the stress out of the holidays.

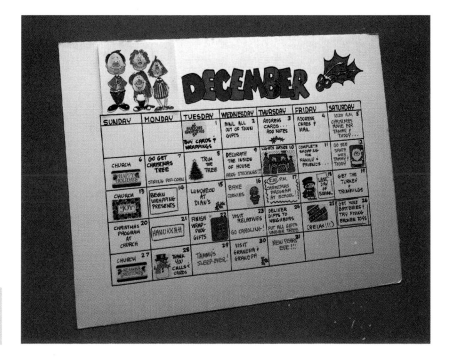

CHRISTMAS IS COMING!

Christmas Memory Makers

Christmas traditions are handed down from generation to generation, but sometimes new ones can be especially meaningful to your family.

WISH BOOK

This clever book will simplify Christmas shopping for the whole family. Using a medium-sized notebook, make a divider for each person in the family. Each person's section includes a page for clothing sizes, items needed, and items wanted.

Decorate the notebook with fabric, wrapping paper, or contact paper. When Christmas (or birthday) present suggestions are needed, one glance at the book, and you can select the perfect gift. Compare notes so several people don't buy the same gift.

Keep the notebook in a location accessible to all family members and use it year after year. Make year dividers at the end of the notebook to keep last year's pages. You'll enjoy looking back at them as the years pass.

CHRISTMAS STORY TIME

Read a favorite Christmas story together as a family after dinner or before going to bed each night in December.

ORNAMENT KEEPSAKE

Give each child an ornament every year. When they leave home and start their own traditions, they will already have the beginning of a collection.

FAMILY NATIVITY PAGEANT

Put on a nativity pageant, complete with the baby Jesus, Mary, Joseph, wise men, camels, shepherds, donkey, and the heavenly star. If your family is small, invite a neighbor family to join you.

CHRISTMAS ELVES

Each week in December, have each person draw the name of a different family member. Do secret acts of kindness for that person during the week.

FAMILY CHRISTMAS BOOK

On separate pieces of paper, have each person record a favorite memory about each of the other family members. The written memory should be about something that occurred during the past year, and might be a shared experience, a kindness done, a good attribute noticed, or an amusing anecdote. Collect all of the papers and preserve them in your Family Christmas Book to savor in years to come.

TAPED STORIES

Personalize a storybook for a young child by recording it on tape. As you come to the end of each page, pause a moment and ring a bell or tap a glass with a spoon to signal that the child should turn the page.

PRESENTS

Rather than opening gifts in a grand melée, open one present at a time while everyone watches. It's sometimes fun to wrap something quite small in a very big box.

Another fun family tradition can be started with a white elephant gift. The person who received it last year secretly chooses a new person to surprise this year. This can be really fun as the gift changes hands each year.

POP CAN ORNAMENTS

Decorate your Christmas tree with fun animals from Noah's Ark!

Aluminum soda pop cans or small juice cans
Metal primer or matte-finish enamel spray paint
Colored enamel spray paints (including flesh color)
Acrylic paint (white, red or pink, blue or green, and black)
Liner brush
Sponge
Clear spray varnish
Scraps of felt or fun foam
Twine
Pipe cleaners
Fringe
Pom-poms
Small hats, bows, and bells
Glue gun

Wash the can and remove the ring. Push the remaining piece of tab back into the can with a screwdriver. Don't put your finger in the hole since the sharp edge will cut!

Crush each pop can by squeezing it slightly in the middle and stepping on one end of the can to smash the ends

together. If you want both ends to show, fold it in half and then smash it from the side. Spray the cans with metal primer or matte-finish spray paint. Follow with the desired color of enamel paint. (Allow each layer of paint to dry before painting the next.)

Using acrylic paints, draw eyes, nose, and mouth. Paint the cheeks on with a small sponge. For the eyes, dip the end of a large brush (or a pencil eraser) in white paint and touch the can to form a large circle.

For the center of the eye, use the tip of a medium-sized brush and add a dot of blue or green. When dry, add the black pupil. Each eye is highlighted with two small white dots. Using a liner brush, outline the eye and draw eyelashes and whiskers with black paint. Spray with a clear varnish.

Cut the ears and legs out of fun foam. Make tails out of twine or pipe cleaners. Use fringe for the lion's mane. Add miniature pom-poms or fun foam for noses. Decorate with small hats, bows, bells, etc.

"Deck the Halls" for Christmas

Take a ride through your neighborhood and explore others in your town to find unique outdoor decorating ideas.

Sketch clever ideas with colored pencils. It's easier to make changes on paper! Make a list of items you'll need—outdoor and indoor lights, spotlights, garlands, cutouts, extension cords, remote controls, etc.

TOPIARY CHRISTMAS TREE

Using gold-foil-wrapped candies will give this tree an elegant touch!

1" dowel (2-1/2 times the height of the pot)
White paint
Red plastic tape
Plaster of Paris
Decorative tin or terra-cotta pot
  (about 7" in diameter)
5" Styrofoam ball
2 pounds individually wrapped
  candy such as peppermints,
  toffee, or saltwater taffy
Straight pins with heads
2 yards (2" wide) French-wired
  ribbon
Christmas floral picks
Spanish moss

Paint the dowel white and wrap it with red tape for a candy-stripe effect. Mix the plaster of Paris according to package directions. Fill the tin or terra-cotta pot half full of plaster. Center the dowel in the pot, pushing it down in the plaster to the bottom of the pot. Add enough plaster around the dowel to fill the pot to within 1" of the rim. Hold the dowel in place until the plaster begins to set up and the dowel doesn't lean. Let the plaster harden completely.

Push the Styrofoam ball securely down onto the dowel. Starting at the bottom, pin the candy (through the wrappers) to the Styrofoam ball. Overlap the candy as you work up the ball, placing the candy pieces together snugly so that the pins and Styrofoam don't show.

When the ball is covered, tie the wired ribbon in a bow and attach it to the top with pins. Trim with Christmas floral picks and tie another wired ribbon around the dowel at the base of the Styrofoam ball. Fill the top of the container with Spanish moss.

Your Christmas Tree

Choosing the perfect Christmas tree is almost a ritual in many families. You might have specific traditions involving:

- When to put up the tree
- Where you buy it . . . a lot or tree farm
- What variety of tree
- Whether to buy a live tree, a cut tree, or an artificial tree
- When and how you decorate it
- When to take it down

If you buy a precut tree, be sure it is fresh. When you get home, cut an inch off the trunk and place it in a large bucket of water overnight. Keep the stand full of water through the holiday season.

Don't burn your tree in the fireplace since the oily soot may cause a chimney fire. Many towns have recycling stations where you can take your tree to be mulched.

Genuine topiary trees are living trees trained and cut to grow in fanciful shapes. Elegant topiary trees were fashionable in early Roman times. Topiary's popularity was at its height during the Renaissance when gardens were filled with elaborate topiaries cut into geometric shapes and animal forms. Make a seasonal topiary for your entryway by attaching fresh or artificial evergreens to a sphere of Styrofoam or chicken wire and decorating it for Christmas.

ANGEL GIFT BAG

This angel is easy enough for little cherubs to make!

Pink lightweight posterboard
1/4" wiggly eyes
Permanent marker (red)
Acrylic paint (pink)
Sponge
1 white (or colored) paper bag
1 (6"–8") round paper doily
White or multicolored curling paper ribbon (hair)
1/2 yard (1/2" wide) ribbon
Small bell
Stapler
Scissors
Glue gun

The angel came to the lowly shepherds to proclaim the birth of the Savior. The message of "on earth peace, good will toward men" rang through the heavens.

To make the face, cut two identical circles from the posterboard, using a 4"–5" diameter can or other round object as a pattern. Glue on wiggly eyes and draw a smile on one posterboard circle. Sponge paint pink cheeks.

Place the gift in the bag. Fold the doily in half and place it over the top of the bag, matching the fold with the bag edges. Staple the center of the doily to the bag. Glue the two circles together, sandwiching the fold of the doily about halfway up the head. Curl several yards of the curling paper ribbon and cut it into varying lengths for the hair. Glue the curled paper ribbon around the face and on the back of the head for hair.

Thread the ribbon through the bell and tie the ribbon in a bow. Glue the tied ribbon and bell underneath the chin.

Red is the primary color of Christmas. It was first used by faithful Christians to remind them of the blood which was shed by the Savior for all people of the world.

Green is the abundant color of nature. The deep green of the fir tree is the second color of Christmas. The stately fir's needles point heavenward and remain green all year round, depicting the everlasting hope of mankind.

REINDEER SWEATSHIRT

Children can make one for each family member.

Light-colored sweatshirt
1 (18" x 24") piece of lightweight cardboard
Masking tape
*Contact paper stencil (8" x 11" or larger, depending on
   shirt size)*
*Fabric paint (light brown, dark brown, red, white, black,
   and green)*
Paintbrushes
5 sponges (face, ears, nose, cheeks, and eyes)
Permanent black marker (mouth and eyebrows)
White distilled vinegar (in a spray bottle)
1/2 yard (2" wide) plaid ribbon
Small bell
Small safety pin

This is a "hands on" project, so wear paint clothes. Allow
each layer of paint to dry before applying the next.

Place a piece of cardboard inside the body of the sweatshirt
to keep the paint from bleeding through to the back. Tape
the arms to the back, pulling the front of the shirt smooth.

Cut an oval out of the center of the contact paper to make a stencil for the reindeer's face. Remove
the backing and place it on the front of the shirt, leaving enough room above the oval for handprint antlers. Smooth the contact paper flat on the shirt. With a sponge, completely paint the oval
light brown, brushing from the stencil edge to the shirt. Carefully remove the stencil.

Squeeze dark-brown paint on your hands and rub them together until the paint totally covers your
fingers and palms. With fingers apart, place your hands at the top of the oval and press firmly to
make antlers. Use alcohol to remove the paint from your hands.

To make the face, cut a sponge into an almond shape and stamp light-brown ears onto the shirt
below the antlers and to the sides of the oval face. For the nose, cut a 1-1/2" round sponge and
stamp a red nose in the middle of the face. For cheeks, cut a quarter-sized sponge circle. Mix a
small amount of red and white paint to make pink, and stamp cheeks onto the shirt at the sides of
the nose.

Cut small ovals from a sponge and stamp white eyes onto the shirt. Make smaller green circles
inside the white eyes. Dip the end of a brush in black paint and dot a pupil in the center of the eye.
Make highlights for the cheeks, eyes, and nose with the end of a brush dipped in white paint. Draw
a mouth and eyebrows with a black marker.

When completely dry, set the paint by spraying the painted area with vinegar, then place a brown
paper bag over the painted area and iron with a hot iron. Thread the bell in the center of the plaid
ribbon and tie it into a bow. Pin or hand stitch the bow at the reindeer's neck.

REINDEER GIFT BAG

Special delivery from Rudolph!

2 sheets brown fun foam (antlers)
1 brown paper bag
1 (2") red pom-pom (nose)
Acrylic paint (pink)
Sponge
1" wiggly eyes
Permanent marker (black)
1/2 yard (2" wide) plaid ribbon
1"–2" bell
Small sprig of Spanish moss (optional)
Holly berries (optional)
Glue gun

To make the antlers, trace your hands on fun foam. Cut out the antlers and glue them to the top of the bag. Glue the pom-pom nose in the center. Sponge paint pink cheeks. Glue on the eyes and draw the mouth with a black marker. Make a bow from the ribbon and glue it to the bottom of the bag. Glue the bell onto the ribbon. Glue Spanish moss and holly berries between the ears.

REINDEER ANTLERS

Make a set for everyone in your caroling party.

1/2" thick foam
Electric knife
Brown spray paint
Puff paints with glitter
Holly leaves and decorations

Measure the circumference of your face—around the top of your head and under your chin. Using this measurement as a guide, draw an oval the circumference of your face on the foam. Draw another circle 2" larger around the first, and draw antlers on the top. Cut out the circle for the face and the antlers.

Spray paint both sides brown and let dry. Outline the edges of the antlers with puff paint. Add holly leaves and other decorations and wear like a hat.

Christmas Cards

Christmas cards strengthen the link between friends. The earliest holiday greeting cards were messages that the Egyptians included with their New Year's greetings in the 6th century. Engravings and woodcut prints appeared in Europe by the 15th century, but Christmas cards didn't become popular until the 19th century when cheap, efficient color printing methods and low postage rates made them affordable.

Take some time this year to personalize your cards. Include snapshots taken throughout the year of special family events. Make a collage of family photos and have it color duplicated or printed by a local printer. Send your child's handprint stamped with green fingerpaint. Potato-print a starry night or make a Pop-up Card (see May).

CHRISTMAS FAMILY TREE

This is an enjoyable project for the whole family!

1 (24" x 48") neutral colored cotton rug (size may vary)
Pencil
Scissors
Contact paper
Plastic plates (to be used as palettes)
Acrylic paints (recommended:
    DecoArt Dazzling Metallics)
    Green (Green Pearl)
    Teal (Teal Pearl)
    Red (Bright Red)
Sponges or sponge brushes
Puff paints or permanent markers
Stencils (optional)
Yardstick
1 yard rope or ribbon for hanger
Artificial holly, bells, and ribbon
Glue gun

Wear old clothes and protect your work area with a drop cloth or newspapers. Draw a large tree-shaped triangle lengthwise on the rug. Cut contact paper into enough circles or ornament shapes for each family member and place them decoratively on the tree.

Pour green and teal paints next to each other on a plastic plate. (Using two colors adds depth and texture to the tree.) Have each family member dip his hand in the paints. Starting at the bottom, fill in the tree design by stamping handprints onto the rug with the fingers fanned out and pointing down from the top of the tree. Move up the tree, using smaller handprints near the top. Help younger children by holding their wrists while they stamp their handprints.

Remove the contact paper. Cut sponges the same size as the contact paper ornaments. Dip the sponges in red paint and stamp ornaments onto the rug in the outlines left by the contact paper. When the paint is dry, stencil or paint your family's last name, the date, and family members' names and birth dates.

Cut a yardstick to fit across the top and hot glue it to the back of the rug. Glue a rope or ribbon hanger to the top. Tie small bows of narrow ribbon and hot glue them to the ornaments. Trim with artificial holly and jingle bells.

Unusual Christmas Stockings

Personalize your stockings!

SPORT AND HOBBY STOCKINGS

Decide on a theme for each family member's stocking. Consider interests, sports, hobbies, and personality. Some examples might be stockings shaped like a golf club, tennis racquet, baseball bat, stamp, horse, dog—even a sewing machine or computer! Make the stocking in the shape of the item which represents the person's theme. Cut out two shapes from felt, sew the sides and bottoms together, and apply Velcro to the opening. Add decorations, trims, and the person's name.

FLANNEL STOCKINGS

Dad's old flannel shirts or mix 'n match flannel can become a *crazy-patch* stocking. Trim the stocking cuff with buttons.

REGAL STOCKINGS

Make stockings with velvet, velveteen, or silk remnants and trim with lace and metallic trims or charms.

Money Gifts

Use one of these ideas to give your $ gift more value!

MONEY SHOWER

6 to 8 yards ribbon or yarn
12 bills of different denominations
Removable tape
Umbrella

Cut the ribbon or yarn into 12 pieces of various lengths. With removable tape, attach $1, $5, and $10 bills on the end of each piece of ribbon. Open the umbrella and tie the ribbons to the spokes. With the umbrella upside down, close it so that the money is tucked inside. What a surprise when the umbrella is opened!

CASH CARNATIONS

12 bills of different denominations
12 (24") lengths of florist wire
Craft leaves
Florist tape
Tissue paper
Long-stemmed rose box
Baby's breath
Floral greens
Ribbon

Accordion pleat the bills in small folds. Fold a wire in half around the center of each bill. Wrap the wire with florist tape, adding one or two leaves as you wrap. Place tissue in the bottom of a long rose box. Lay the cash flowers in the box and add baby's breath and floral greens. Tie the box with colorful ribbon.

DOUGH DUMP TRUCK

Toy dump truck
Ribbon
15 rolls of coins

Fill the dump truck with rolls of coins and trim with a ribbon.

MONEY CATERPILLAR

7 to 8 rolls of coins
1 piece (4" x 36") green felt
1 yard large yellow rickrack
Thread
1 (3") pom-pom (head)
1 pair wiggly eyes
1 small red pom-pom (nose)
1 yellow pipe cleaner (antennae)
4 yards yellow ribbon
Glue gun

Fold the felt in half lengthwise. Sandwich rickrack between the edges on the long side, allowing the rickrack to show. Stitch 1/4" from the edge to make a casing for the coins. Stitch one end closed. Glue a 3" pom-pom head to the closed end. Glue the eyes and a red pom-pom nose to the 3" pom-pom. Bend pipe cleaners to make antennae and glue to the felt. Fill the felt casing with coins and tie a yellow bow between each roll and at the tail.

HOLIDAY SKATES

1 pair old ice skates
Masking tape
Spray metal primer
(gray) or gesso
Matte spray paint
(burgundy)
Acrylic paints and brushes
or Christmas wrapping
paper decoupage
Clear varnish
4 yards gold or silver ribbon
or braid (narrow enough
to lace skates)
Florist wire
Pine cones
Red dried flowers or berries
Florist Bow
Wire for hanging
Gold or silver glitter spray
Glue gun

Clean the skates and remove the old laces. Cover the skate blades with masking tape. Spray the skates with primer or brush on gesso until the skates are completely covered. This could take several coats.

When dry, spray with burgundy spray paint and allow to dry. Remove the masking tape. Tole paint with acrylic paints or cut Christmas designs from wrapping paper or cards, and decoupage onto the skates. Spray with a clear varnish. Lace the skates with gold or silver ribbon or braid. Attach the skates to a pine swag with thin florist wire, so that the wire is concealed.

Wrap florist wire around the pine cones and attach the cones to the pine swag. Hot glue small dried flowers or berries to the swag. Make a large Florist Bow and wire it to the top. Make a wire loop on the back to hang. Lightly spray with gold or silver glitter spray.

The bow on a gift is to remind us of the spirit of brotherhood that ties us together.

Florist Bow

This bow is a festive finishing touch for all kinds of projects.

Allow 3 yards of ribbon for a large bow. With your left hand, pinch the ribbon about 8″ from the end, leaving an 8″ tail. With the right hand, twist the ribbon at this point over to the "wrong" side, scrunching it tightly together.

Make a 1″ loop with the "right" side of the ribbon up, twisting it underneath the loop to the wrong side. Pinch it tightly and hold it with your left hand.

To continue making loops for the bow, twist the ribbon over to the wrong side again and make a 3″ to 4″ loop. Twist the ribbon over to the wrong side again and make a loop for the other side of the bow, twisting and making loops until you have 7 to 9 loops on each side. The trick is to hold the twists tightly in your left hand while you continue to add loops with your right hand. Leave an 8″ tail.

Secure the center of the bow by wrapping a 6″ piece of thin wire around the ribbon you are holding in your left hand, threading it underneath the 1″ loop and catching all of the center twists of the loops. Twist the wire tightly at the back and use the extra wire to attach the bow to your project.

Adjust the loops to stand out evenly and to hide the wire. Trim the tails on the diagonal or with a "V" wedge. Voila!

POTTED CANDLE

Terra-cotta pots can be festive candle holders.

Terra-cotta pot
Plaster of Paris
Candle (twice the height of the pot)
Decorations such as buttons, seashells, clear or polished stones,
    crumpled metallic paper, crumpled metallic thread,
    nuts sprayed with gold paint, sequins, garlands
Ribbon
Glue gun

Mix the plaster of Paris according to package directions. Fill the pot half full of plaster. Center the candle in the pot, pushing it down to the bottom of the plaster. Add enough plaster around the candle to fill the pot to within 2″ of the rim. Hold the candle in place until the plaster begins to set up and the candle doesn't lean. Let it harden completely.

Decorate the pot and around the candle with any of the decorations listed above. Spray flammable materials with flame retardant. Don't leave the lighted candles unattended.

ICE CANDLE HOLDER

Light the sides of your walk on Christmas Eve.

Plastic ice cream bucket or other container
Heavy plastic glass, large enough to hold the candle
Gravel
Duct tape
Large candles

Fill the bucket with water and place it in the freezer. When the ice in the bucket is partially frozen, fill the plastic glass with gravel and place it in the center of the ice to make a hole for the candle. If it won't sit flat, tape it down with duct tape. Freeze solid.

Turn the bucket upside down and dump the gravel into another container. Fill the glass with cool water to thaw the ice just enough to remove the glass. Remove the ice from the bucket and place a candle in the hole.

If the temperature stays below freezing, this sparkling candle holder will last outside for several days. It can also be used as an attractive centerpiece placed on a platter to catch the water as it melts. Decorate with pine boughs, holly berries, and pine cones.

The flame of the Christmas candle is symbolic of man's gratitude for the star which appeared in the heavens at Christ's birth. In the early Christmas celebrations, candles were placed on the trees. Colored lights on the tree now signify the star.

165

GINGERBREAD COTTAGES

Enjoy this project, but save some candy for the cottage!

1 recipe Gingerbread
Christmas candies, jelly beans, and candy canes
1 or 2 recipes Royal Icing (see April)
Wafer and Lorna Doone cookies (shutters and doors)
Necco candy wafers (roof)
Peanut brittle, Oreo cookies, or orange sticks (paths)
Sugar cones and gumdrops (trees)
Pastry bag with decorator tips

Cut and bake Gingerbread according to directions. Separate the candies into muffin tins so they are easily accessible. Ice everything that requires white icing first, and tint the rest of the icing as needed.

Join one side wall to an end piece by piping icing along one edge and pressing the end of the other piece into it. Prop the pieces at right angles so they stay together until they are dry. Allow the icing to dry thoroughly before handling the pieces.

When the first two pieces have hardened together, attach the other end piece or wall. Allow the walls to dry before adding the roof. The assembled house should dry overnight before it is decorated. Attach doors, shutters, roof tiles, and cookie and candy trims with tiny dabs of icing. Landscape with paths, trees, and lots of snow.

Making a gingerbread house is a perfect family activity for a cold December night. Gingerbread creations can be so simple a five-year-old can make them, or so exquisitely crafted that they become showpieces. Let your imagination guide the decorating, and you'll be surprised at how easy it is to produce enchanting cottages.

GINGERBREAD

Nothing makes the holiday air smell quite so wonderful as the aroma of fresh gingerbread!

Patterns (from lightweight cardboard)
1-1/2 cups butter or margarine
2-1/4 cups brown sugar, firmly packed
1-1/2 cups dark molasses
1/2 cup water
7 to 8 cups all-purpose flour
1 teaspoon salt
1-1/2 teaspoons baking soda
7 teaspoons ground ginger
4 teaspoons ground cinnamon
2 teaspoons ground cloves
2 teaspoons ground nutmeg
1 teaspoon ground allspice

Photocopy or trace the pattern outlines with tracing paper and enlarge. Transfer onto lightweight cardboard using a dull pencil and carbon paper. Cut the patterns with a matte knife or sharp scissors.

In a large bowl, cream the butter and sugar. Add molasses and water. In a separate bowl, mix all the dry ingredients together. Add the dry ingredients to the wet ingredients, a cup at a time, and mix on low to avoid "fluffiness." If the dough is too stiff for your mixer, mix it by hand with a metal spoon or with clean hands. Divide in half, wrap in plastic wrap, and refrigerate 2 to 3 hours.

Preheat the oven to 350°F. Roll out the dough 1/4″ thick on waxed paper or parchment sheets. Dust the pattern pieces with flour, lay on the dough, and cut out. Leave the pieces on waxed paper or parchment and place on cookie sheets. Allow at least 1/4″ between pieces.

The dough may also be rolled directly on a lightly greased foil-lined baking sheet. A piece of plastic wrap on top of the dough keeps you from having to add flour. A damp towel underneath the baking sheet will keep it from slipping. Cut around the shapes, and remove the excess dough.

Before baking, cut the windows and doors, but do not remove the cutouts. Recut after baking. Windows can be removed from the warm gingerbread, but do not remove the doors until the gingerbread has cooled thoroughly, and then remove them carefully. When constructing your gingerbread house, the door can be positioned open, so you want it to be flat and unbroken.

Bake cut shapes for 10 to 15 minutes for larger pieces, and 8 to 10 minutes for smaller pieces. Gingerbread should be firm and lightly browned to ensure a rigid cookie that will stand up without bending.

Remove the gingerbread pieces from the foil, lifting them firmly, but with care. Peel off any remaining foil or waxed paper. Store the pieces in an airtight container until you are ready to assemble them. They may absorb moisture from the air and soften.

Cookies meant for eating should be rolled 1/16″ or 1/8″ thick, and baked until they are lightly browned at the edges. Makes two 14″ x 16″ rectangles, 1/4″ thick.

(Note: You may substitute mace, cardamom, or pumpkin pie spice for the allspice and nutmeg. For the best flavor, use spices that are less than one year old. If you have a spice grinder, freshly ground spices are wonderful!)

Cut one pattern with door and one without door.

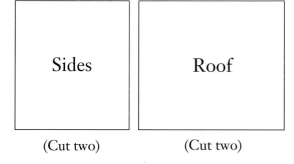

(Cut two)   (Cut two)

Gingerbread

Gingerbread is probably the oldest cake in the world. It was famous throughout the Mediterranean area as early as 2800 B.C. and became popular in England when the Crusaders returned from the wars. In the 1600s, gingerbread bakers had the exclusive right to make gingerbread, except at Christmas and Easter.

During the reign of Queen Elizabeth I, gingerbread structures were often made to celebrate special holidays and feasts. Some weighed as much as 150 pounds!

GINGERBREAD GARLAND

Hang this garland by the front door and snip off a gingerbread treat for visitors to munch on their way.

1 recipe Gingerbread
Small gingerbread man cookie cutter
1 recipe Royal Icing (see April)
Pastry bag with decorator tips
Plastic wrap
1/4" ribbon
3 yards plaid ribbon for Florist Bow

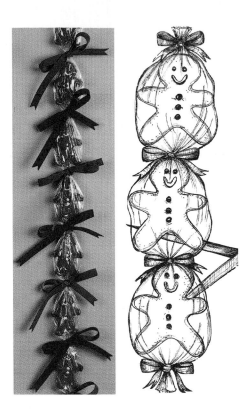

Prepare and roll out the gingerbread. Cut out gingerbread men with a small cookie cutter and bake. Decorate with Royal Icing. Cut a length of plastic wrap the desired length of the garland, and lay it out on the table. Place the decorated gingerbread men face down lengthwise on the plastic wrap, about 2" apart.

Fold the plastic wrap in from both sides, overlapping it to securely cover each gingerbread man. Tie a bow with 1/4" ribbon between each gingerbread man, and top the garland with a large plaid Florist Bow.

GUMDROP TEDDY BEAR

Decorate your Gingerbread House with some of these playful bears.

2 large gumdrops
7 small gumdrops
3 whole cloves
1/4 yard (1/8" wide) ribbon
Royal Icing (see April)
Round sugar cookie (for name-card holder)
Ornament hanger and paper clip (for ornament)

Fasten the flat ends of the 2 large gumdrops together with Royal Icing. Make arms and legs by attaching small gumdrops with icing. To make the bear's muzzle, cut a small gumdrop in half and attach the flat end to his face.

For ears, cut 2 gumdrops in half and stick them to the sides of the head with icing so that the flat side is against the head. Use whole cloves for the eyes and nose, and half of a small gumdrop for the tail. Tie a ribbon around the neck.

To make a name-card holder, make the bear so that his legs are stretched out in front and he looks like he's sitting. Attach him to a sugar cookie with Royal Icing. Make a tiny name card to sit on the bear's lap and attach it with icing.

To use the bear as an ornament, stick a small paper clip down into the head, with 1/4" of the end loop showing. Hang with an ornament hanger.

STRING SNOWMAN

This lightweight *Frosty* is simple to make.

2 inflated round balloons (body and head)
1 cup sugar
1 cup hot water
Crochet-cotton string
1 (1") red pom-pom (nose)
Black felt (eyes)
Red felt (mouth and scarf)
Green felt (mittens)
Top hat
Glue gun

Follow the directions for making the String Basket (see April). To construct the snowman, cut away the string around the top of the largest ball so that the smaller ball fits snugly into the top of the large ball. Glue the balls together. Cut and glue the features onto the face. Trim with a red felt scarf, top hat, and mittens.

POPCORN SNOWMAN

Making this jolly snowman is an indoor family activity!

1/2 cup butter or margarine
1 (16 ounce) package miniature marshmallows
20 cups popped popcorn
Vegetable oil spray
Small black top hat (available at craft stores or make
  your own out of felt or paper)
Candy or nuts
1 (1" x 14") strip of red felt

Melt the butter and marshmallows on low in a saucepan or microwave and pour over the popcorn.

Spray your hands with a vegetable oil spray. Form the popcorn into three balls—small, medium, and large. To secure the balls on top of each other, form a well in the top of the large and medium balls and a corresponding bump on the bottom of the medium and small balls so they nest on top of each other.

Decorate the snowman with a top hat, and use candy or nuts for the face and buttons. Make a jaunty red scarf for his neck out of a strip of felt.

COOKIE EXPRESS

Dry ice makes the Cookie Express engine spout steam!

1 recipe Royal Icing (see April)
1 large package Oreos
1 large package sandwich waffle cookies
1 package oblong cookies
2 packages Lifesavers
3 cotton balls
5" wire
Gray or black spray paint
Small candies or dried fruit to fill cars
  (red hots, M&M's, raisins, etc.)
Black string licorice
Orange sticks
Pastry bag with decorator tips

ENGINE

Stick 4 Oreos together with Royal Icing for the engine's hood and set aside.

To make the cab, stick 3 sandwich waffle cookies together, one on top of another. Turn them so they are standing vertically. Stick 2 oblong cookies onto the sides of the waffle cookie stack.

The chassis is 1 waffle cookie laying flat. Stick the Oreo hood on top of the chassis and put the cab behind the hood.

Cut a waffle cookie in half and set it under the car to prop it up while you attach 4 Oreo wheels. Stick a Lifesaver onto the center of each Oreo. Remove the half cookie when the icing on the wheels is dry.

For the smokestack on the engine, stick 4 Lifesavers together and stick to the engine's hood. For smoke, push 3 cotton balls onto a 5" wire and lightly spray with gray or black spray paint. Put a small amount of frosting into the Lifesaver smokestack and push the wire down into the Lifesavers.

Pipe frosting onto the middle section and around the Oreo wheels. Pipe a window onto the sides of the oblong cookies.

For Christmas entertaining, place a small dish behind the train and fill it with small pieces of dry ice. Pour hot water over the dry ice and watch your steam engine Cookie Express come to life!

The star represents the heavenly sign of promise. God promised a Savior for the world and the star was a sign of the fulfillment of that promise. The countless shining stars at night, one for each man, now show the burning hope of all mankind.

COOKIE CARS

To make a cookie car, cut one waffle sandwich cookie in half for the two ends. Place a whole sandwich cookie on the bottom and stick 2 waffle cookies on the sides. Stick 2 oblong cookies on the outside of the whole waffle cookies.

Prop the car up with half of a waffle cookie underneath while sticking the Oreo wheels in place. Put icing onto the Lifesavers and stick them to the center of the Oreo wheels. Remove the waffle cookie half when the icing holding the wheels is dry.

Pipe icing around the top of the car. Repeat this step until you have as many cars as desired. Fill each car with cargo such as small candies, raisins, or orange sticks.

CABOOSE

For the caboose, stick 3 waffle sandwich cookies together. Stand them vertically and stick 2 oblong cookies onto the sides.

Prop it up with half of a sandwich cookie underneath while you stick an Oreo onto each side for a wheel. Stick a lifesaver in the middle of each wheel. Pipe a window onto the side of the caboose and pipe frosting around the middle.

TRAIN TRACK

To make the train track, run 2 licorice strings on the table, 2″ apart. Place orange sticks every 3″ to 4″ for railroad ties. Place the train on the tracks.

Wrapping gifts in unique home-crafted wrap adds a personal touch to any present. Even younger children will enjoy making or receiving specially wrapped gifts. Cut 1/2″-thick sponges into Christmas shapes using cookie cutter patterns. Dip the sponges into tempera paints and apply to plain brown or white paper.

More elaborate gift wrap is easy to make using ordinary materials such as shelf or brown paper, tissue, leaves, and paint. Paint or trim wrapping papers to match the color and theme of your Christmas decorations. For elegant paper, make designs with oil-based or metallic paint using a paintbrush or sponge. Spray the tops of partially dried maple leaves or ferns with metallic spray and allow to dry. Spray the undersides with adhesive and stick them to the paper. Allow all papers to dry thoroughly before using and store them flat to avoid cracking.

THE 12 DAYS OF CHRISTMAS
The Romans celebrated the feast of the "Invincible Sun" on December 25, but in other areas the winter solstice was associated with January 6. As Christmas was combined with the winter solstice celebrations, over time, the celebration was divided between December 25 and January 6. The pre-Christmas season of Advent was one of quiet preparation, and the festivities belonged to the 12 days between December 25 and January 6.

VEGETABLE CHRISTMAS TREE

You can vary the trimmings for this tree with an assortment of brightly colored vegetables.

Leaf lettuce, curly endive, or parsley
Olives, cherry tomatoes, mushrooms, carrots, radishes
Pieces of yellow pepper
1 large Styrofoam cone
Clear plastic wrap
Florist clay
Elastic bands
Wooden toothpicks
Decorative toothpicks (with colored cellophane ends)

Wash the vegetables and dry them, either on paper towels or in a salad spinner. Cover the Styrofoam cone with clear plastic wrap. Attach the cone to a serving plate with florist clay.

Starting at the base of the tree, wrap leaves of lettuce or parsley to completely cover the cone, attaching the greens with toothpicks or elastic bands. Arrange the leaves so that they look like evergreen branches. Attach the last few leaves at the top with wooden toothpicks.

Attach the olives, cherry tomatoes, and mushrooms with decorative toothpicks. Use a tiny cutter to cut the yellow pepper and carrots into fancy shapes. Make radish roses by making thin slices in a circle to within 1/4″ of the base of the radish. Place the radish in cold water for the rose petals to flower out. Cut a star out of the yellow pepper or make a radish rose for the top of the tree.

WASSAIL MIX

Keep this mix handy during the holidays to warm up unexpected guests.

4 cups Tang
1 cup Country Time lemonade mix
2 teaspoons ground cinnamon
1 teaspoon ground cloves
1 teaspoon ground ginger
6 (1 ounce) packages spiced cider mix
1/4 cup sugar

In a large bowl, thoroughly mix all ingredients. Use 2 to 3 tablespoons of mix per 1 cup of hot water. Serve or package in a Christmas tin as a gift. Makes about 6 cups.

The steaming beverage we know today as wassail originated from the Middle English *waes haeil*, which means "be thou well" or "to your health." Spiced ale and beer were served during the holidays to warm chilled bones.

172

SANTA HEART COOKIES

This versatile sugar cookie is ideal for a cookie exchange!

1 cup butter
1-1/2 cups sugar
1/2 teaspoon salt
1-1/2 teaspoons vanilla
3 egg whites
3-1/2 cups all-purpose flour
1 teaspoon baking powder
Buttercream Icing
Chocolate chips (eyes)
Red hots (nose)
Gumdrops (mouth)
Coconut (mustache and beard)
Plastic wrap
Heart-shaped cookie cutter

BUTTERCREAM ICING

Vary the flavor and colors of this versatile icing to complement the cookies.

3/4 cup butter, room temperature
3 cups powdered sugar
Pinch of salt
3 teaspoons vanilla extract
2 teaspoons orange extract
1 tablespoon milk
Paste food coloring

In a medium bowl, beat butter, sugar, salt, vanilla, orange extract, and milk until fluffy. Divide into separate bowls and tint with food coloring. Spread or pipe on cookies. Makes about 3 cups.

Cream butter, sugar, salt, and vanilla. Add egg whites and blend. Stir in flour and baking powder until well mixed. Form into 2 balls, cover with plastic wrap, and refrigerate several hours or overnight.

To bake the cookies, preheat oven to 350°F. Roll a ball of dough 1/4" thick. Cut out the cookies with a heart-shaped cutter and bake for 6 to 8 minutes or until very lightly browned. (Baking time depends on the size and thickness of the cookies. Watch them carefully.) Cool on a rack.

Make Buttercream Icing and divide into 3 bowls. Tint one red, one white, and one flesh-color. (Flesh-color can be made by mixing red and yellow.)

Turn the cookie so the point is at the top. To make Santa's hat, pipe icing on the top (pointed) 1/3 of the cookie. To make the face, spread flesh-colored frosting on the lower 2/3 of the cookie. Use chocolate chips for the eyes, a red hot for the nose, and gumdrops for the mouth. For the beard and mustache, sprinkle coconut around the edge of the heart and over the mouth.

With white frosting, pipe fur across the edge of the red hat and add a pom-pom on the point. Makes about 5 dozen (3") cookies.

(Note: This cookie can also be frosted with Royal Icing.)

The candy cane is symbolic of the shepherd's crook. The crook on the staff helps bring stray sheep back into the flock and represents the helping hand we should show at Christmastime.

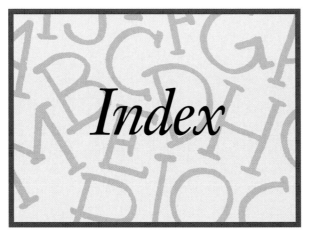

H

I

J

K

L

Have Fun with Dian Thomas!

Americans are finding their greatest pleasures at home. Enjoying their families. Entertaining their friends. And they're looking for ways to do it easily and inexpensively. Dian Thomas has been showing America how to do just that on national television for more than 20 years! She's been a regular on ABC's *Home* for six years and NBC's *Today* for eight years, and she has also appeared on *Tonight*, *Donahue*, *Sally Jessy Raphael*, and *The Tom Snyder Show*. She delights audiences with her innovative—and sometimes zany—ideas. Now you can get in on the excitement. Choose from Dian's complete assortment of books and videos then **LET THE FUN BEGIN!**

◄ HOLIDAY FUN YEAR-ROUND

Dian Thomas treats you to a year's worth . . . many years' worth . . . of fun. In *Holiday Fun Year-Round*, you will find exciting ideas that turn mere holiday observances into opportunities to exercise your imagination and turn the festivity all the way up!! *Holiday Fun Year-Round* is a collection of decorating ideas, crafts, activities, and recipes. You'll discover interesting tidbits of information about how each holiday came to be, why we observe it, and how to celebrate it with gusto.

From New Year's to Christmas, *Holiday Fun Year-Round* is loaded with magical ways to make your holidays special. Dian's ideas are winners! 192 pages, full-color photos. **$19.99**

◄ ROUGHING IT EASY

Even the camp cooks have fun when they're *Roughing It Easy*! This *New York Times* best-seller is chock full of recipes and great ideas that make outdoor camping and cooking an adventure. It is the complete camper's bible. Cook eggs and bacon in a paper bag or boil water in a paper cup, and even start a fire with steel wool and batteries! There are suggestions for equipment selection, fire building, campfire cooking, and even drying your own foods for backpacking! If you love the out-of-doors, *Roughing It Easy* is for you. 248 pages. **$14.99**

◄ FUN AT HOME WITH DIAN THOMAS

This collection of creative ideas, demonstrated on ABC's *Home* show, has something for everyone. Dian shows you how to entertain with originality, keep the kids busy on a sunny or a rainy day, cook in your fireplace, and craft mundane household objects into unique decorations. *Fun at Home with Dian Thomas* is full of practical, easy ways to add fun to everyday living. Ideas range from a zoo full of inexpensive foam rubber toys for the kids to garage organization. It's a treasure of fun do-it-yourself or with-your-children projects! 208 pages, over 500 illustrations. **$14.95**

TODAY'S TIPS FOR EASY LIVING

Today's Tips for Easy Living is about adding zest and sparkle to your life. From her appearances on the NBC *Today* show, Dian shares over 400 great ideas for today's time-strapped families. She has tips for quick meals, stay-at-home vacations, homemade toys, novel party ideas, kids' treats, household hints, and more. 160 pages, 265 color photos. **$12.95**

DUTCH OVEN COOKING BASICS VIDEO

Dian Thomas, an avid Dutch oven chef, is your guide to learning everything you need to know about getting started with Dutch oven cooking. She walks you step-by-step through the process as she energetically prepares delicious recipes and shows unique ways to use your oven.

Filmed in Utah, the heart of Dutch oven country, this video gets down to the very basics of Dutch oven cooking. Helpful tips take the viewer through oven selection, seasoning, cleaning, and storing. 30 minutes. **$9.95**

FUN AT HOME VIDEOS

Creating Fun & Easy Toy Projects
Quick & Easy Holiday Ideas
Let's Party!

Each video gives you step-by-step instructions and patterns for unforgettable party ideas, holiday decorations, and fun toys! 30 minutes. **$9.95** each.
